In and Against the State

In and Against the State

The London Edinburgh
Weekend Return Group
A Working Group of the
Conference of Socialist Economists

Pluto  Press

First published November 1979
by the London Edinburgh Weekend Return Group
Reprinted May and July 1980
This revised and expanded edition
first published November 1980 by Pluto Press Limited,
Unit 10 Spencer Court, 7 Chalcot Road, London NW1 8LH

ISBN 0 86104 327 8

Designed by John Finn
Cover photograph: Peter Harrap (Report)
Photoset and printed in Great Britain by
Photobooks (Bristol) Limited, 28 Midland Road,
St Philips, Bristol

Contents

Acknowledgements

We would like to thank the many people who have helped in the preparation of this book. Most of all we are indebted to the sixteen people whose description of their predicament forms the basis for the first chapter and many of whom gave us additional help with the postscript. They gave their time to talk to us, to read the transcripts and help work out a reasonable representation of their feelings. A further, more extended group took time to read the drafts and help us to make the book better and clearer.

We acknowledge our debt to everyone who helped and encouraged us.

Preface to the Second Edition

When we wrote the pamphlet *In and Against the State* we called it 'Discussion Notes for Socialists'. We hoped that it would be part of, and bring a new dimension to, the process of building ideas about how to work towards socialism.

There has been discussion, debate, criticism and support. We have been encouraged by the fact that people have found our ideas important enough to spend time talking about them, arguing with them and working to clarify them. It seems that *In and Against the State* has succeeded in speaking to people's experience. The response to it has confirmed that this is part of the socialist struggle where new ideas and forms of action are needed.

We have decided to republish *In and Against the State* for a number of reasons. It has given us the opportunity to deepen our understanding of the ideas we are putting forward, and to bring them up to date: to develop them in the light of the deepening crisis and the rapid changes now taking place in the way the state affects and controls people's lives. And it has allowed us to respond to the discussion and criticism of the pamphlet which has taken place.

We do not go from pamphlet to book without reservations. We have discussed at length the political issues involved in changing the form of presentation and distribution. The size and layout of the pamphlet, its price, and most of all the photographs, which we feel often say as much as the words, will be lost. And we are aware that by going through a professional publisher we give up our collective production and financing of *In and Against the State*, and remove the work of distribution from PDC (Publications Distribution Co-op), whose setting up of a socialist collective in this field we feel is important.

In the end, we have chosen to publish through Pluto: we feel that this will mean that *In and Against the State* will reach a different and wider group of people and, more important, it will ensure its continued availability and distribution over a longer period of time.

We have made only minor alterations to the original text, trying to clarify it in areas where there has been misunderstanding, and to simplify our ideas where they have been confusing or confused. It is in the Postscript that we have attempted to develop the discussion.

We recognise that *In and Against the State* speaks directly of and to only one group of state workers. Its main message is about the frustrations, contradictions and opportunities experienced by the more 'professional' state workers—teachers, social workers, advice workers, nurses, DHSS workers. We said in the preface to the first edition what kind of work we do and have done, and the pamphlet of necessity came largely out of our individual and collective experience.

We understand, perhaps even better for having written this work, that the everyday experience of and problems facing manual and low paid, clerical and industrial state workers will in many ways be different from ours. But we believe that the basic point we are making is relevant to those workers, as it is to all workers, whether in the state sector or private industry. It is essential to find ways of working for change from within our jobs and our private lives; ways of developing effective, organised oppositional action which comes directly out of the everyday oppression we experience.

London Edinburgh Weekend Return Group
Summer 1980

Preface to the First Edition

We are a small group of people who work for the state or for organisations which receive money from the state. We are socialists. We believe that the struggle for socialism includes a struggle against the state—one in which we, as state workers, hold a key, and at the same time contradictory, position. If we are to work in and *against* the state, we must find ways of bringing the struggle for socialism into our daily work.

The class position of some state workers is clear. Many public sector manual and clerical workers are the lowest paid of all employed people. for others it is equally obvious: they are highly paid management staff, top civil servants, directors of nationalised industries. But what about nurses, teachers, social workers? Their position seems ambiguous.

Those of us writing this book fall into the middle group of workers, who are often termed 'professional'. We are social/community/advice/research workers. Often these types of jobs might seem as though they were above class. But our jobs have become increasingly disciplined, especially since the cuts in public expenditure which are pushing us all into positions and attitudes that are similar to those of workers for private capital.

We do not want to make some easy assertion that we are working class. That overlooks the real differences between people's oppression, for class derives from all sorts of hidden advantages and disadvantages as well as our jobs. But, the changes in the jobs that we do over the last 15 or 20 years have brought us like thousands of others in similar jobs to see ourselves as part of the working-class movement. Like many others we have made a choice. If we don't choose to be part of it, we inevitably choose to work against it. The point of this book is that we choose to be part of the struggle for socialism *within our own jobs* by the way we do them. We write from within our own struggle, the struggle against the state.

Some of us are women and feminists. For us the struggle to

change relations within society is not just against capitalism but against sexism as well. The subordination of women by men existed long before capitalism, but is reinforced by the capitalist system and the state. The fight for a change in the relations between man and women must go hand in hand with that for socialism. It cannot be assumed that sexism will automatically disappear in a socialist society.

In our group some of us are tenants, some are parents, all, at one time or another, have been patients. We know we have no choice but to enter into routine relationships with the state to obtain money, resources and services. We depend on and are controlled by state provision, rules, demands. As 'clients', too, we feel the need to organise to fight against the state.

The state is not neutral. It does provide services and resources which most of us need—education, health care, social security. But it does not do so primarily for the good of the working class. It does it to maintain the capitalist system. Although the state may appear to exist to protect us from the worst excesses of capitalism, it is in fact protecting capital from our strength by ensuring that we relate to capital and to each other in ways which divide us from ourselves, and leave the basic inequalities unquestioned.

We believe that it is essential that capitalism be seen not just as an economic system, but as a set of social relations. It determines the way we see ourselves and others, the way we treat each other, the way some people have control over others' lives.

The state, too, is more than a structure which administers numerous services and programmes. It is a complex set of social relations which must be maintained if capitalism is to 'continue'. It is characteristic of the state that it treats us as individual citizens, families, communities, consumer groups - all categories which obscure class. By this process, the state seems to define us and our problems in ways which confuse us. It helps hide the fact that it is the *capital relation* which is the root of our problem and shapes our lives. The state also establishes a hierarchy of power and decision-making. This hierarchy is one of class, but it includes the subordination of women and people of certain races and religions. These groups have a special experience of state oppression and must sometimes organise autonomously as well as together with other parts of the working class.

Those of us who work for the state are inevitably part of the state. We must find ways to oppose it from within our daily activity, which means breaking out of the social relations in which the state involves us and creating alternative forms of organisation as we struggle for socialism. If we do not, whether we recognise it or not, we are perpetuating a capitalist society – one which is exploitative, sexist and racist.

Struggle against the state – against the social relations it perpetuates – goes on all the time. The state is an often frustrating and threatening part of our daily lives, and struggle against it is instinctive. But it is often individual, risky and ineffective. Struggle must be collective. It is important that we understand what forms of collective action will most effectively challenge the state form of relations and provide a basis for building socialism, and then organise ourselves around them.

Because parties and trade unions on the whole have devoted little attention to the problem of how a state worker's hours of employment can be directed against capitalism and towards a transition to socialism, we have found that when we join them we are limited to 'after-hours' socialism. We spend our evenings and weekends struggling against capitalism, and our days working diligently as agents of the capitalist state to reproduce the capitalist system. Like Penelope, in the Greek myth, we stitch the tapestry of bourgeois society every day and attempt each night to unravel it before dawn.

Is there any way out of this hopeless dilemma? Can we shape our daily activity in such a way as to avoid stitching capital's tapestry, can we hinder rather than promote the reproduction of capitalist social relations? Does the fact that our work is situated in the state give us special opportunities in this respect, or is that merely a reformist illusion? These are the issues that we want to discuss. The aim of this book is to provide a framework for that discussion.

We first look in detail at the predicament people feel they are in, as state workers or as 'clients' and subjects of the state. Then we look more directly at the state itself. What is its part in capitalist society, how has it developed in recent years, how has it responded to crisis and change, and what difference has that made for us? In particular, we emphasise that the state is not just a set of institutions, but a pervasive form of *relations*. Finally, we consider the shape that working-class struggle against the state has taken, ways in which people have seen and seized opportunities to oppose, to challenge the state form.

The Conservative Government elected in summer, 1979, is apparently attacking many aspects of the state, cutting state expenditure yet further, causing the loss of state jobs. This confuses many people who feel the need to defend the state, yet do not feel that it is 'their' state and know that the state itself oppresses them. It is all the more urgent, therefore, that as socialists we look for ways of fighting back oppositionally, rather than simply defending a state we know to be indefensible.

London Edinburgh Weekend Return Group
Autumn 1979

1: **In the State**

Many people have started talking about such institutions as schools, hospitals, local councils and local magistrates courts as 'the state'. Yet just a few years ago it would have seemed quite out of place to most people to use such a hard, 'political' term about such familiar, everyday things. In seeing such institutions as part of 'the state', we are also asking questions about the state in Britain today. Is it helpful, or neutral, or oppressive to us? How can we influence its actions? And so on.

These questions arise because more and more of us, in more and more ways, are closely tied up with the state's institutions. Take an average working woman with children. In the mid-19th century her sole contact with the state would have been the Poor Law Guardians and the police. Today such a woman has dealings with the education authority over her children's schooling; with the doctor and the hospital over her own and her family's health; with the town hall Directorate of Finance over rates; the Housing Department over rent. Besides, she will be visited by the social worker, the probation officer and possibly the juvenile department of the police, over her kids' street life; Inland Revenue over her earnings; the Unemployment Benefit Office or Social Security if unemployed. She may well approach an Industrial Tribunal over her unequal pay, or a Rent Tribunal over her unfair rent. In addition it is likely that at some stage in her life she will have a job in some public organisation, because about a third of all people in jobs today are employees of the state—whether as cleaners of buildings or roads, caretakers, clerks, cooks, social workers, architects, teachers, doctors or administrators.

A distinction is often made between our public and our private life. But even the parts of our life designated private do not any longer, if they ever did, seem to be fully under our control or unaffected by the state and its policies. The state seems at times to penetrate even our closest relationships with each other. Apart from the fact that the state marries and divorces us, officialdom has a well-defined view about 'the family', and what it should be.

Relations between men and women and their children are relevant to state institutions, they appear to matter to the authorities. Men are designated 'head of household' and have certain rights and duties. Women, as housewives and mothers, are expected to carry out, to a certain standard of proficiency, many jobs that the state also has a hand in, such as training children and nursing the old and sick. Women whose husbands have died are treated differently, receive different benefits, from women who are divorced or separated. The imbalance of power and initiative which women have suffered is rooted in the home, in the relations of sex, child-bearing and domestic work. But this imbalance doesn't stay within the confines of the home – it has spread out to influence the world outside, the world of work and business and of the law, administration and welfare. Women are sometimes noticing and pointing out that their experience with the state (as employees or 'clients') is in some ways an extension of the disadvantages they experience in private life.

The state also influences how we relate to our workmates, our bosses, those above and below us in the hierarchy. It determines in part how much our employers can pay us, whether or not we will be made redundant. It puts limits on ways in which we can organise and take action as workers. It affects the way we relate to those we come into contact with through our work – our 'clients'. This is especially true if we are state workers.

Our experience of the state is contradictory

The ways in which we interact with the state are contradictory – they leave many people confused. We seem to need things from the state, such as child care, houses, medical treatment. But what we are given is often shoddy or penny-pinching, and besides, it comes to us in a way that seems to limit our freedom, reduce the control we have over our lives. The tenant of a council house, pleased enough to obtain a tenancy, could still say plenty about inadequate maintenance and restrictive rules and regulations, for instance. As state workers, perhaps voting Labour, we may have hopes that a Labour administration is in the working person's interest. Yet we find that, as manual workers employed by a Labour-controlled council or government, we are as overworked and underpaid as we would be in a private firm.

As workers in those occupations that are termed 'professional', such as social work, or teaching, we are often given impossible problems to solve arising from poverty or from the powerlessness of our 'clients'. The resources available to back up our intervention – the welfare provision of the state – are a drop in the ocean of need. And besides, it is clear that many other actions of the state and of the economy itself are pulling in the opposite direction, making things worse for the poor. We often feel that we are being asked to manipulate people, to use women's pride in their home or love of their children, for instance, as well as their need of the practical resources we partially control and can give them access to, to induce co-operation.

As socialists we're always taught that somehow services provided by the state are better than those from the private sector. Better be in the hands of a council than a private landlord; better our NHS than extortionate private medical insurance schemes – and so on. And this seems to be true, but only up to a point. Somehow what we get is never quite what we asked for. The waiting lists for hospital beds were always too long; gradually charges began to be introduced for this and that. Another example is the promise of the new towns after the war – which made Britain famous for town planning, but were somehow, when it came to it, bleak social deserts to live in. It is not just that state provision is inadequate, under-resourced and on the cheap. The way it is resourced and administered to us doesn't seem to reflect our real needs. Pensions, for instance, seem to be maintained at a level, and given on terms, that have little to do with the way *we* experience our old age. They seem geared more to the needs of employers or the state.

State provision leaves a bad taste in our mouths. State institutions are often authoritarian, they put us down, tie us up with regulations. And many of the working class seem to be defined by the state as 'irresponsible', as 'troublemakers', 'scroungers'. If we are born out of wedlock it defines us as 'illegitimate'.

All these things leave us wondering: if the state is not providing these services in the way we want them, it cannot really be doing it for *us*. Why does the state provide them?

Deepening contradictions

A few years back, in late 1975 or early 1976, the long-threatened contraction of state expenditure began in earnest. The pruning of services and the abandonment of capital building programmes only took effect gradually. But it has become increasingly clear to us that assumptions many of us made in the sixties about 'the welfare state' were mistaken. Our hopes and demands for general improvements had always been perverted into 'special case', selective welfare – inadequate and with strings attached.

The Labour Party has always promised to be a party of 'reform'. Even those who felt reform was either not enough, or a misguided route to socialism, were at least confident that economic growth combined with working-class pressure would ensure a gradual improvement in standards of housing, of health, of education. People now gradually became aware that the 'cuts' signified not a short-term set-back in a general curve of improvement in standards, but a reminder that the term 'welfare' has always been ambiguous.

The cuts and the fight-back against them, however, have raised useful questions in people's minds. Perhaps it never was *our* welfare state? We are still, somehow, certain that it is right to fight against the sale of council houses into owner-occupation; to fight against turning medicine over to private practice; or the de-nationalising of the steel industry. But perhaps we should not be looking to defend the state, even the 'welfare' state, as it is, but fighting for something better? If so – how do you get what you can, defend yourself against losses, and resist oppressiveness, when losses and gains seem to be two faces of the same coin?

When we first started to write this we already felt that, drawing on our own experience as state workers and as 'clients' of the state, we had a clear and painful idea of the predicament in which the state catches us. We wanted to fill out our understanding of it, however, by long conversations with people in different kinds of situations. We decided to include here quite substantial reports of what they told us – because we were amazed by the sharpness of the contradictions people were experiencing, the clarity of their observations and the imagination they were applying to finding a political solution.

The conversations are not put forward as evidence – but as illustration. The people chosen and the kind of relationship they are in with regard to the state, are not an ideal selection and do not cover, or even represent, every facet of our interaction with the state. We recognise that they under-represent manual jobs, for instance, the bulk of state employment. They do not include clerical work. And they don't express the special predicament of black people, and other groups (Ulster Catholics for instance) up against the state. Nor do they reveal the oppressiveness of the state's definitions and practices on homosexuals.

★The first conversation was with Maureen, a woman who has raised a large family, needing the state for her income. For her, the state seems to give independence with one hand, while stealing it away with the other.

★The second conversation was designed to raise some of the contradictions in which state manual workers find themselves. We talked to John, about the situation of a conductor on London Transport buses.

★Sarah, Neil, Patrick and Mary are teachers, aware that state education is oppressive in many ways, but each trying to find a way of teaching what they feel is right.

★Joan and Kate work for a Community Health Council. They know that their job for the state is to channel protest into manageable forms, but they talked about the ways in which they found they could use their position to support the struggle for better health.

★The fifth conversation we had was with a number of workers in two community advice centres, overwhelmed with requests for help with housing and other problems, but trying to develop collective and class-conscious forms of organisation in their area.

When we talked to people we made it clear that we ourselves were socialists, and in the case of the state workers we chose them because they were socialists too, asking them about the limitations and possibilities of their position.

Finally, we had a meeting with three Labour Party activists. Two of them were backbench Labour councillors in a Labour-controlled local authority, hoping to use their position to push the Labour leadership to radical policies in support of their working-class constituents. They are a different case from the others we talked to, in that they chose their position precisely for what they felt it could offer a socialist. In this they contrast with a state employee, who may justly say that she or he needs the job and the pay.

The accounts that follow deal mainly with the problems people experience, and in this way they may seem rather depressing. But we felt it important not to skimp on spelling out the contradictions carefully, so that the difficulties should not be underestimated when we later go on to examine the possibilities of finding a way around them. The discussions did lead to constructive and positive ideas about ways of acting as socialists and as feminists in relation to the state and these hopes will surface again later in the book.

Maureen

Maureen Murphy lives in south London and has had ten children, all but one now grown up. Her husband died nine years ago when the youngest was six. She has lived her life and brought up her children by means of careful, painstaking dealings with a set of official institutions. Among them, the most important are social security, the housing authority, the health services, the education system and the police and law courts. But it would be possible to list a dozen more types of official with whom she has dealings.

The state is far more important to Maureen than any boss from whom her husband ever earned a wage. So she has never gone out of her way to have a fight with the authorities. 'It doesn't get you anywhere. You don't win. They have the majority every time. You can go down to the council and rant and rave, you still won't get anything. If you go down and ask in a polite way, then you might get what you want.' She takes care to keep on the right side of them. After all, 'They are important to me these people. I do have to depend on them. I can't afford to take risks.' This good reputation is particularly important because Maureen believes that there is a connection between the various official bodies. 'If you get into trouble with one, the other one is likely to know. That is what I think, anyway.'

The family has been dependent for many years on social security. She reckons that she normally gets what is due to her, but occasionally appeals against decisions. 'About money for Eileen's shoes, for example. I filled in the little blue slip and explained why they were necessary for her.' She got the extra allowance without going to a tribunal. Social security don't visit now, don't bother her. 'They know me.'

As far as housing goes, the family has been with the council for 36 years, mainly as GLC tenants. She now has a good rehabilitated house. 'They give me no bother.' But neither do they do repairs. She accepts this as a matter of course.

She and her children have grown familiar, through one crisis after another, with many nearby hospitals: Kings, St. Thomas's, Guys, Great Ormond Street, the Belgrave, the Evelina. Maureen herself has asthma and bronchitis now, and is subject to heart attacks. Her youngest daughter is mildly epileptic. The children have had many alarming illnesses and accidents. One had pneumonia, another polio. One dropped a match in a petrol tank and had serious burns on the face. Another gashed her leg on a steel bar while playing on a bomb site, and had 32 stitches. Maureen became practised in dealing with the health service and with her own worry. 'You get used to it. It just grows on you. It's like going and doing the shopping every day.'

She learned what things were serious enough to warrant going to the big teaching hospitals. But she preferred the small local children's hospital, the Belgrave, now threatened on account of the cuts in government spending. 'They were very kind to the children there. Eileen had an operation on her head there. It's a very very good hospital. A lot of women here really use it. You can go in and give the children their lunch and tea. The Evelina was like that too, but it's been closed a long time now.' GPs however have not really been much use to the family. 'I don't know of any good ones. The doctor across the road, he'll write me a prescription, but he never asks how you feel. He's overworked. He needs seeing to himself.'

So crucial is the state health system to Maureen's family that the strikes of ambulance men, doctors and nurses are moments of real worry for her, for fear of having nowhere to turn. 'I just say afterwards, thank goodness it passed this time without anything happening.'

The school system has been a problem to all Maureen's children. Most of the kids spent a lot of their childhood staying away. School could never hold their attention. Eileen, being epileptic, had a specially hard time in the year she spent at the local comprehensive. 'She just stood outside the classroom door. She wouldn't go in. She just wasn't able to mix with people at all. She learned nothing there.'

Then Great Ormond Street hospital, to Maureen's relief, said she ought to send Eileen to a special school. She was able to use the health system as a lever on the education system. They got her a place. But only after a year of waiting. And during that year Eileen was continually at home in Maureen's care. 'You see, I didn't really want her to go out alone, you never knew when she might have a fit.' This real additional responsibility for Maureen was caused by a school that had no time or money to spend on an unhappy girl. The work of caring and coping can be passed backwards and forwards in this way between the state and a woman at home.

The comprehensive school was too big. 'There's too many children. They can't cope there. They are just not able to run after every child.' Maureen had had a formal meeting at the outset with too many different teachers. After that her only contact with the school was through letters. She does not remember ever having had an invitation to any kind of social event, or to a chat with an individual teacher.

The 'special school' to which Eileen was eventually sent was not so meanly resourced. It was an ideal school in Maureen's eyes. 'The headmaster was ever so nice. And then, parents could go there for all the outings. They'd tell you all about the school and show you round. There would be Christmas parties and open days. Eileen is taken and brought back each day on the bus. She has the same teacher all the time. They give her her tablets at lunch time. And if she isn't well, they will ring me and tell me. They are very interested in her. She likes it so much she is going to stay on, though she could leave this summer.'

Because the comprehensive schools failed to hold the children's attention, they were continually being picked up by the authorities. The local policeman, whom Maureen knew and respected as the copper on her beat, would come round and warn 'If Eileen doesn't go to school she'll end up in trouble.' In spite of several appearances in court, though, she has never had any of the children taken away. But the threat of the law is always a worry.

One aspect of the welfare state that many of her friends are involved with is social services. Maureen has steered clear of social workers. 'I had social workers or probation officers at one time, when the kids were in trouble. I never hit it off with them.

Everything you tell them, you know, it is supposed to be confidential. But they write it down. I knew a girl working down the office and she said "I've seen your records". Well, that put me off completely. Anyway, I don't think they have anything to offer. One of my boys was always taking and driving cars. This social worker says to me "What do you think the answer is?" I told her "I don't know." She says, "I don't know either." Well, I mean, they are people who are supposed to know about education. If they don't know the answer, how can I? So, when I was offered a social worker after that I turned it down. I felt I couldn't have that aggravation again, always being put down and everyone reading your notes.'

Maureen contrasts her life and relationship with the state sharply with her mother's experience, a generation before. Her mother, who died recently aged 92, brought up her family in an Irish village. Her husband was more of a responsibility than a help, having been ill from the age of forty. So she used to take in washing. 'You had to pay for the doctor so we didn't go. We just tried to get better. That's how it was. There were no benefits then, only the pension when you were 70. The only trouble we ever got into was to pinch fruit from someone's orchard. All they would say to us was "you'd better get off or I'll let the dog out after you." The magistrates court was meant to open once a month but it seldom did. If there was a case, it was someone caught without a bicycle light, or someone letting their cows wander in the road. So my mother never worried about us getting into trouble. Nobody would ever take you away, or anything like that. That never happened.'

It seemed to us, talking to Maureen, that the present day provision of a free health service and supplementary benefit would make today's state seem preferable to her, compared with the state as her mother had experienced it. After all, social welfare has enabled her to bring up her family without depending on a man or his earnings. Even when Maureen's husband was alive it was she who had mainly kept the family going. 'He was never indoors much. He never wanted the responsibility for the children.' She wouldn't, in any case, have wanted things different. 'I wouldn't have wanted to be domineered.' And it is the welfare state that has made this small degree of independence possible for the first time. But to Maureen even these advantages do not seem to quite outweigh the power that the state has over you—especially the power to remove your children from your care. 'It's worse for me than it was for my mother,' she said, emphatically.

Maureen was also in no doubt that the state, as she and her family recognise it, is something that has a special concern for and a special relationship with women. It is something that singles out women in the family for its dealings, and which women know most about. 'I learned how to handle it better. It applies to quite a lot of women.' Maureen hasn't done a regular paid job, she has had no other work than the relentless 24-hour occupation of looking after children, now in its second cycle with growing grandchildren. But handling the institutions of the state has been for her a kind of work. On the quality of the relationship she can sustain with the state's institutions depend her income, her home, her own and her children's health and prospects, and her self-respect.

Working on the buses

Until recently, John was a bus conductor. He did the job for three years, after six or seven years in clerical and accounts work in another nationalised industry. He is a socialist and involved in an anti-racist organisation. He did not suppose, however, that working for the state had some kind of merit for a socialist. He expected that this 'public service' job with London Transport would be no more worthwhile or rewarding than a job for a capitalist firm. And he was proved right.

In London Transport, basic pay is low. It is supplemented by extra payments for unsocial hours and for split shifts. A split shift may be, for instance, four hours on the job and four hours off, followed by a further four hours on. Payment is made for the time off. This work pattern does, however, make a mess of the day. Even after this the wage is still inadequate and many drivers and conductors work overtime. This means working one of their two weekly 'rest days'. They are not allowed to work both, as it is against the union agreement. The way the work is organised is unsatisfactory too, because it divides the workers up. 'There may be five hundred people working out of one garage, but you tend only to see your own team and those on the same shift. Shift changes are frequent. Many people in the garage you won't see at all.'

There is a lot of stress in the job. 'You are the person who has to take the brunt of the irate public for the bad service and high fares.

That aggravation does wear you down. It becomes a two-way hostility. There is an hour's gap between buses, say. The people get angry. They have a go at you, and you hit back, though you know your interest and theirs is really the same. It is that bad feeling that gets people down.' But possibly the strain on drivers is worse. 'The stress of driving in London has really increased in the last fifteen years. There are juggernauts, more traffic generally.'

Conductors are at the bottom of a hierarchy of management. Their work is supervised by inspectors of several grades. 'You are meant to show respect to inspectors and carry out their instructions. They are like foremen. They think they are your boss. They try and pull rank on you. They go through a distinctive sort of training and wear a special uniform. There are the ones with a silver badge, and they have no turnups on their trousers. The ones above them, with a gold badge, do have turnups. These are the inspectors responsible for either route controlling or checking fares on the bus.' There are others in the garage (who don't wear uniform at all), responsible for schedules and supervision within the garage. 'One of the things they do is check up on whether you are wearing your uniform. If you are wearing jeans they'll say "Where are your grey trousers?" If you say, "I didn't fancy wearing them today" the inspector will report you and send you to the garage manager. If you do it several times you may have to go up to Division. And if you have a few times late they start looking at your record.'

As well as uniformed inspectors, London Transport employ plain clothes spies, called 'spots' by the drivers and conductors. 'These "spots" are meant to be checking up on the passengers to see if they dodge payment of the fare, but they also check up on the conductors to see they are not pocketing the money. For instance, if there is a certain stop where people are likely to be getting off after a short ride when the bus is busy, they may hand the fare to the conductor on the platform and not wait for a ticket. A "spot" will place himself strategically on the pavement just opposite such a stop to see if the conductor pockets the cash.'

Above the inspectors is the Garage Manager, and above him the Divisional structure. There hierarchy is both sexist and racist. 'Although there is no legal impediment to women drivers or inspectors, you still find a few of them. The number of women drivers is token, and when they are taken on it is probably because they can't get the men. And there are fewer black drivers and conductors.'

With this management system weighing on you, and a long working week for little pay, there is no feeling of commitment to a public service. For the majority it is just a job. 'It is not surprising really. Apart from the job itself, there is the whole ideology being put over to people that state firms are inefficient, unprofitable, and paid for at the tax payer's expense. State industries or services like London Transport are run on the same basis as private industry, with the workers having no say or control, so how can people in them have a view of their job as worthwhile and useful? Why should they?' So people don't stay in the job long. The turnover is high. Only a third stay for five years or more. And there is a shortage of about a thousand drivers and a thousand conductors in London Transport. 'People are aware, the public, that they wouldn't do that job. People know what the state of the buses is. You have to be pretty desperate to do it.'

Those who do take on the job of driver or conductor are so alienated by the conditions, the stress and the niggling supervision, that they engage in a sort of guerrilla warfare against the terms of work. 'It is an everyday struggle. If you want to be, you can be awkward. If the bus is not clean when you start, or an indicator light is not working, you can officially use this as a reason not to take it out.'

John described the kind of low-level sabotage that bus teams engage in. 'They might let the tyres down. Or run slow, by getting into a slow lane. Sometimes there is deliberate "bunching", when several buses on one route follow immediately behind one another. Although in most cases "bunching" is a result of traffic or other factors, when this happens crews might then take advantage because they feel like having an empty bus or an easy ride. Or people may leave five minutes before schedule to get longer for a cup of tea the other end. And you can make things bad for an inspector, if he makes things bad for you. If he sees you coming by 15 minutes late and doesn't turn you round you can delay 20 minutes the other end and come back even more behind hand, which causes him a lot of trouble. All these things make the service worse for the passengers. But they are really secondary. Basically, it is that there are not enough buses on the road, they are in disrepair, and there are not enough spare parts. It is a bad service.'

The service has deteriorated considerably over the last twenty years. 'There were 42,000 drivers and conductors in London

Transport. Now there are about 20,000.' The cuts in public expenditure, more recently, have had a serious effect both on the service to the passengers and on the working conditions of the employees. 'They have cut the fleet by 10 per cent. They have rationalised the schedules. Some routes have been cut out altogether, and more are to go soon. Some they have made shorter. The thing is that shorter bus routes are useless, they won't pay their way. And in six months' time they will turn round and say "These routes are unprofitable". They will show the figures and the workers will have to agree they should be scrapped.'

The introduction of the one-man bus (in which the conductor's job is scrapped and the driver controls the doors and collects fares) is part of the GLC and London Transport attempt to rationalise the service. The results of this have been loss of jobs and a worse service. 'The introduction of one-man buses was a defeat for bus workers. Ever since their introduction in the late 1960s, the service has steadily been destroyed. Where there does appear to be more service to the public, it has been fiddled off the workers,' John said.

'They are cutting out the split shift. On the surface this might seem to be an improvement, but people used to be paid for the interval between shifts. Now they are adding the time onto six or seven-hour jobs to bring them up to eight. The aim is to give us a standard 40-hour week. The management is getting tighter. Gradually over the years it has been getting more like the management of a private business.'

'The tactic over the cuts has been divide-and-rule. One garage suffers cuts in routes and jobs, and another may gain a bit. Each garage becomes concerned in fighting to save its own jobs.' At an individual level, too, the workers are divided against each other. 'The introduction of one-man buses means a loss of conductors' jobs, and more stress for the driver. But the drivers who get those jobs (and there is no shortage now of people ready to take them) get 25 per cent higher pay than the rest. So resistance gradually dwindles away.'

The union that represents the London Transport conductors and drivers is the Transport and General Workers Union. Its current stance is entirely defensive. In fact, its principal demand is for more, not less exploitation. 'The struggle is to increase the amount of overtime available to the workers – instead of fighting for a better service for both employees and passengers.'

When London Transport introduced Bus Plan 'cuts' in 1978 they presented it to the union as a fait accompli. 'The union opposed it, but not on principle. They just took a stand on LT's "failure to consult". We engaged in short strikes during the rush hour. That did cause London Transport to negotiate with the union, but there were no major concessions, no reversal of the position. Just a bigger compensatory settlement, and the cuts phased over a longer period – 18 months instead of a year. Incidentally, 87 per cent came in during those strikes, and 13 per cent stayed out on the road. Those who did were nearly all one-man drivers.'

History has a bearing on present struggles. The last big strike on the London buses was in 1958. It was over pay, and it lasted six or seven weeks. The London Underground workers did not strike in support, however, and the bus workers finally failed. They went back to work for less than they had demanded. This means that they entered the present 'cuts' offensive already weak. And the offensive, far from uniting the workers and passengers against the state, has driven more wedges between them. As the service deteriorates, the conductors pick up the abuse. Fare increases, fewer buses, delays, are all taken out on the conductor who is caught between the transport management system and other sections of the working class.

'Should the conductor take it into his own hands to break the limit of five people standing in the bus and let more people in? In a way it is in our interest, as conductors, to do that, because we get a £1 commission for every £46-worth of fares we collect. And the five-person limit is a trade union limit. By law we can carry up to nine. But if you cram people on it is dangerous, it is difficult to do your work, and, besides, it takes away the pressure for more buses, which is what we all really need.'

The more the pressure brought to bear on the passengers and the workers from a deteriorating service, the more they resent each other. 'Many conductors are irritated by old age pensioners, who are allowed to travel free between certain hours in London. It was the best bit of legislation brought in by a Labour GLC, in my view. But it is more work and more worry for the conductors. They call OAPs "The Wombles". You see, they move slowly. You need a bit of patience. But you are in a hurry, there is pressure to get on. It is one more aspect of tension in the job. I think OAPs should travel free all the time, but there are resolutions in our union branch saying they should be stopped, because it is impeding people's journey to work. Instead of demanding extra buses.'

There is considerable danger to conductors from assault by angry or drunken passengers. One in ten each year get attacked at some time or another. 'The irony of the situation lies in the fact that the better you do your job from the management's point of view, the more you are officious, the more likely you are to get beaten up. You should be able to do what they want of you, at least, without running the risk of getting hurt. Many assaults also result from the bad service. Disgruntled passengers go further than just verbal abuse, they sometimes use physical violence.'

The problem is that when bus workers do take action to defend themselves against the state, they hurt the public even more. 'It hits the people you want to be in solidarity with. And next day you get the abuse. You are really prone to angry passengers. There is need to get more involvement, to politicise people on the buses. But the high turnover of workers makes it difficult.' Limited strike action also hurts colleagues. 'If there is a strike on one garage area, other routes carry the burden of extra passengers. When ideas are put forward in the union suggesting action that would hurt the working class less and the state more, such as refusing to collect fares instead of refusing to take the buses out, the bus workers think it is utopian and unpractical. They see the struggle in economic terms. "If we don't collect the fares they won't pay us the increase we are demanding"'.

John feels the union to be bureaucratic and set in its ways. 'Branch stewards and shop committees have been there for years, some of them. Union work is just a routine. It is very difficult to inject politics into the thing. It is a closed shop, so they don't need to go out of their way to involve people actively, to attract people to join, to see some point in it. When you take on the job, all they are interested in is how you are going to pay your sub.'

Yet people have not lost their ability to organise, to relate to each other off the job, and have a good time. London Transport social club is very big and successful, with many facilities all over London. There is a snooker room in most garages, people playing cards together. But no connection exists between this friendly, active scene and union struggles. 'If the union organises a dance about two people turn up.'

Advice centre workers

The first 'law centre' was set up in Notting Hill in the early 1970s. Several others followed within the next few years, first in London, then in the poor inner areas of other big cities. Now there are over thirty in the country. They were often the initiative of socialists, including professional lawyers, who wanted to use their skills to help people in poor areas. They mainly looked to the Home Office Urban Aid Programme for financial support – and so the pattern is now that they are mainly funded by government, part-central, part-local.

In a similar way over the same period there developed less specialised advice centres, concerned mainly with helping people to get information about their rights. Both law and advice centres are situated right on the dividing line between state and non-state – some would say they crossed the dividing line and became official bodies when salaries began to be paid by the government. Certainly the state sees them as part of a policy. They are a manifestation of the 'restructuring' of the state apparatus, described in chapters 3 and 4. The workers however often have a degree of autonomy and their own ideas about how the centres should be run. Their operation is often a daily struggle.

On the whole they have been welcomed by socialists, conscious of the financial barriers which limit working-class access to the legal system and the relatively few lawyers with expertise in employment and social security law, which very directly concern working-class people. Law centres seemed to offer a mechanism for more effective legal redress. But we found that the workers we talked to had no illusions about the law. Far from being a means of improving things for the working class, it seemed to them to obscure the class reality of their 'clients' situation and to lead away from a solution.

The Law Centre workers gave us an example of the kind of situation with which they have to deal. They described a property company, owning flats for rental in their area. 'This company operates on the fringes of the law, with very clever legal advisers. Lots and lots of individual tenants have come in to see us about them. The way the company operates is to make big profits by rehabilitating property and reletting it for higher rent. To do this it has to get sitting tenants out. The tenants are offered alternative accommodation, as an inducement to move. Later they find that the flat they have moved into doesn't really belong to the original company. They are up to all sorts of tricks like that.'

'Our real problem is that the council ought to have bought up the estate in which this company operates. Although the council isn't an ideal landlord and there would still have been problems, they would be problems of a different kind. Far from buying up property, though, our council (which is now Tory) is actually selling off the housing that it does own, which the Labour council before it had bought. So these nasty landlords have a free hand. And the mechanisms for bringing them to book are not very strong. You have to have a lot of evidence to go to court for repairs. And even the strongest tenant is often too scared of the landlord to go through with it. Landlords get away with it nine times out of ten, because the tenants can't withstand the pressures. It is slow, almost impossible, to obtain repairs through the Public Health Acts or Section 32 of the Housing Act 1961. Mind you, through Section 157 of the Housing Act 1957 you can quite quickly get a closing order put on a flat. This means the landlord must put out the tenant. The council must rehouse him. But that means first that someone else is pushed down

the queue. And second, that the landlord, although he is now obliged to repair before reletting, does get vacant possession which is just what he wanted in the first place.'

The Law Centre workers emphasised that this case is quite typical. Their job seems to be to deal with a potentially endless stream of problems caused to the working class by capitalism and the state, such as low earnings, unemployment and stress; inadequate and costly housing and rapacious landlords. The resources the state makes available to them to do this job – a handful of salaries, inadequate or unfair legislation and a tortuous legal process – they feel are derisory.

In response to their understanding of the needs of the poor working class around them, workers in this particular Law Centre moved rapidly away from 'advocacy' work, to helping individuals press their own cases. From there they moved towards organising, where they could, groups of clients to support each other. Today they aim to use advice work as a way of drawing together active groups into campaigns around issues.

There was much in common between the approach of these Law Centre workers and that of the workers from the 'non-legal' Advice Centre who also took part in this conversation. Both sets of workers faced quite difficult choices.

For instance, there is the problem of the 'open door'. There is a flood of cases arriving at the Centre, an expression of profound need in the working-class population of the area. 'It is a real struggle just sharing up the reception duties. We had two full time receptionists, one of whom left after six months due to the strain. We run reception on a rota now, including a 24-hour emergency service. We are very loath to turn away case work. Although we do shut the door increasingly over the years, it doesn't solve the problem because more people come in when we open.'

In some instances, certain tangible gains may be achieved, some wrong righted, by working on any one of these individual cases. Besides, people can learn confidence and progress from defeativeness to anger through pursuing their case as far as it will go. And it is in humanitarian terms hard to turn people away when they ask for help. At a higher level, it is possible, by an accumulation of successful cases, to improve the working of the law, to educate local lawyers in new kinds of work, and so on. Often, however, it is the sheer pressure of numbers that keeps you working at this level.

'I'm so bogged down in casework that I don't even see my way to doing work with groups.'

The workers, however, know that what can be achieved this way is limited. In any case there is no time to respond to all the cases. And it is essentially selective – since some must be chosen at the expense of others and a gain achieved for one person may be at the cost of someone else. It is an 'individualising' procedure in a situation where they see their main role as raising a class consciousness. Above all, they sense that individual casework is precisely what the state wants them to do.

They feel sure that advice centres have been set up in order to direct threatening working-class militancy into acceptable established channels. 'Instead of going en masse to the town hall they come to us one at a time and we go through the procedures. If they say "We haven't enough to live on" we pull out a leaflet and say "Ah, but have you applied for a supplementary grant for heating?" The contradiction lies in the fact that the channels do work, for some people some of the time, and we cannot afford to ignore the possibility.'

Conversely, the workers feel there does exist a possibility of combining cases that arise from similar issues and to work on a dossier, an organisation, a campaign. But people in these working-class areas have no strong tradition of collective action. 'They are not used to being organised in groups. They are very much isolated in their own lives. They are not used to joining in, knowing and extending their rights. They haven't had the experience. They have been sat on all their bloody lives.'

While people act as individuals there is always a danger that they will be forced by circumstances into competing with each other. Even within and between collective groups competition is rife. Organisations, once formed, often fall into rivalry with each other, they become a power play. 'How can it be otherwise, when the whole society is so competitive?' And once practical limited goals are achieved, groups often break up. The competitive ethic even affects community workers, who fight on behalf of their own area against a neighbouring one. 'There was I working slowly in my patch, helping the working class to help themselves, while the community workers in the neighbouring area were charging in, leading campaigns, demanding this and that. As a result they got a phenomenal amount of services and we lost out.'

As one of the workers pointed out, the Urban Aid system itself is set up as a competition between groups. 'All applications go into a bundle, they all go to the co-ordinating voluntary group, you are invited to a meeting and given ten minutes to make your case – to say why you should get the money and not the others. Then there is a discussion, and then you vote. You take on responsibility for the selection.' And it is a method that works in favour of the articulate. 'There is a nursery project in our area, for instance. The person running it doesn't happen to be a very good speaker and can't argue their case very persuasively. It makes me sick, it really does. I mean, we get put through as top priority and get our money, and they don't. You come away feeling so bitter. It's divide-and-rule all the way.'

Internal organisation is a particular predicament for advice centre workers. While they want to organise collectively, sharing money, jobs and responsibility, pressure from the authorities tends to demand a management committee and a director – who is both spokesperson for the group and answerable to the authorities. 'Collective running is clearly threatening to them. They want one person in control so that they can contact that person, make them responsible, sack them if necessary . . .' Both centres have a person who is a good negotiator, a good manipulator, but feel ambivalent about this. 'We see its uses. But we are also very critical of this. It concentrates a lot of knowledge and power in this person's hands and short circuits our collective organisation.'

Events over the past year, however, have intensified the predicament in which workers of both centres find themselves. They operate in poor working-class districts of London, within Conservative-dominated boroughs. Both were set up, in the more permissive political climate of the early seventies, as liberal voluntary sector initiatives. With the arrival of the Tories both centres came under attack. The councils claim they are reviewing the centres' operations to save public expenditure. But the nature of the attack suggests political motivation.

Curbs are being imposed on the way the centres interpret their role. They are forbidden by the council to do political work with squatters, anti-racists, strikers. One has even been proscribed from working with any group criticising the policy of public authorities or political parties – and that includes the National Front. They are required to return to more 'technical' advice work, under the more direct control of the council. Workers are aware that they must either reduce the amount of politically productive work they do, or lose their funding. They also see themselves as having the choice between lying low, in an attempt to save their own centre – or exposing their hand by joining in a strong collective campaign around the closure of similar centres.

The workers feel that there is a contradictory need both to use the law, for what it can offer, and to expose it for its fraudulence. Stepping outside the law, for instance displaying addresses of empty properties in the window, is politically productive; but you risk getting closed down. But then again, if you stay within the law, you may remain secure, but you perpetuate the myth of 'we are all equal before the law'. As living standards fall and the state tightens its managerial control, this contradiction intensifies. Workers are sure that any resources which assist the working class to fight back as law and advice centres can do, must be defended. But the same trends limit their own scope and the fight back must be more and more muted if they themselves are to survive.

Teachers

'Once you go in and close the classroom door you are on your own' said Neil. Behind the closed door the teacher has both a degree of freedom and a degree of answerability for the classroom situation. In this lies the main contradiction that she or he experiences.

For outsiders who are not teachers, the relative freedom of the classroom situation would seem to offer many possibilities for introducing children to new ideas and values and helping them develop a critical awareness of their society. In our meeting with four London teachers, however, we discovered some of the constraints which make teaching in a socialist way not at all easy.

'The teacher is controlled simply by the way the job is set up. They give you the absolute minimum to work with and ask you to do the absolute maximum. There is one of you and thirty children. Classes are too big, books and paper in short supply. You are always juggling with a set of priorities in trying to equip those kids even with a basic set of tools for thinking about the world and assessing what's happening to them.' It is not just the lack of resources, however, nor the high student/teacher ratios which make teaching difficult. The classroom situation itself presents teachers with many contradictions.

On the one hand the socialist teacher wants good relationships with the children, a happy and democratic classroom, one in which 'the power moves away from the front to the back of the room, so that the way you organise your class is different from what the kids think they are at school for and what the school thinks it is doing for the kids,' said Patrick. 'What I would like to do is to encourage kids' confidence in their own voice.' However, 'the model laid down for you is an authoritarian one, in which you are supposed to set out the tasks for the kids. If you don't believe in that, you totally screw up discipline for some time. You have to take a lot of shit while the kids are being re-educated to the new kind of situation. Standards fall to pieces. According to any headmaster or inspector you are just not doing your job.'

That apart, however, 'creating an honest personal relationship that challenges discipline isn't enough', because the resulting chaos makes it all but impossible to teach the things that the socialist teacher herself or himself wants to teach. There was some difference between the teachers we talked to as to what they felt it important to get across. Patrick for instance felt that if you could get the kids to work out what it is they would think if left alone, this would be good in itself. Though he recognised the need to teach basic literacy and numeracy, Neil felt that there was more to socialist teaching than stripping away a veneer of false consciousness to reveal a 'natural' democratic, non-racist, non-sexist child. Something positive has to be offered in his view. Both were agreed however that through chaos in the classroom you may sacrifice the political effect that might be possible through orderly teaching.

The dominant feature in the life of most teachers is the problem of discipline, of control over the kids. It absorbs so much energy and attention that little remains for analysing the system that threw teacher and children into this conflict. In the first instance, the teacher feels as constrained by his or her responsibility to the students as directly by the rules and regulations of the school hierarchy. Mary felt, for example, that there was a conflict between her desire to give the children freedom of expression and the dictates of their own well-being. 'I have to have my kids organised enough that I can get them in two lines safely across the pedestrian crossing outside the school. And that itself is a clear disciplinary constraint on me. If they are overexcited and I can't control them, one could be hurt or killed. The classroom teacher is in an extraordinary position because she is at the bottom of the ladder, but is actually more responsible for the kids than anyone else.'

The problem, however, is much more complicated than just ensuring the physical safety of the children. A major dilemma for teachers is the extent to which they should teach to meet students' and parents' *own* expectations of school (preparation for exams, for instance) as opposed to teaching kids in a way which teachers feel will equip them for the reality they will face on leaving school. 'A lot of those kids are going to fail exams. You don't want to teach them to fail, but whatever you do they are going to. It would be best to concentrate on teaching them to know their own strength.'

In a situation where O-levels are marked by the proportion of pupils officially required to pass them in any one year, and not by the actual standard any one child has reached in the exam, the imperative for socialists must be 'to start to try and teach them why they are failing,' as Neil said. But since the children themselves have naturally adopted some of the same values as the school-and-employment system, this can be very painful. 'I showed a video film' said Mary 'which tried to put across the idea that regional accents and idiom were not inferior to "standard English". The film made the children who spoke "standard English" sound rather ridiculous. The O-level students hated it. They found it extremely painful to hear what they were striving to achieve analysed in that way and perhaps run down.'

The rules and regulations and the expectations of the staff higher up the hierarchy, however, are never far away from the classroom teacher, serving both to reinforce her isolation in coping with the contradictory pressures of the classroom and intervening when things are not going as they should. The delicate trust the teacher builds up with the children can be shattered by a directive from above. 'Last week some child was writing all sorts of rude graffiti on the walls. All tutors had a directive to physically *search* every child in their tutor group to see if they were carrying a blue felt tip pen. It puts you in a terrible position.' The possibility of incursions from above like this hang over everything the teacher does.

'Your low position in the hierarchy determines more than anything else what you can do. Your role is very prescribed really.

Although we play with these ideas of changing our role, there is a very limited range within which you can vary the traditional teaching role. It is because of the whole way the school is organised and your position in it. Take me, I'm a grassroots classroom teacher. I have got a head of year above me, and a deputy; and I am in a department that has a deputy head and a head. These two systems, the year system and the departmental system are cross-cutting. Above *them* there are things like deputy and head of lower school; and finally the Head.'

Mary and Sarah were also very strongly aware of the way in which the subordination of women was part of the hierarchical relationships within the school: Mary felt that quite personal questions were unnecessarily brought into her job interview with the (male) head teacher. 'He asked me if I lived with the father of my child! As if that had anything to do with the way I teach.'

Because ordinary classroom teaching puts teachers under these pressures, many socialist teachers have sought jobs in special units which have small numbers of students and relatively high ratios of teachers. Sarah found teaching in a special unit for 'disruptives' allowed her to relate less formally to students and offered the advantages of team teaching too. Mary and Patrick had had similar good experiences working in an Intermediate Treatment Unit. But they also felt that working on the periphery of the system in this way meant that you did not have so many opportunities to directly challenge mainstream education practice. 'You can do incredible things in that situation, outside this bloody great state machine. But you suspect all the time that you are being used as a dustbin for problems the schools can't cope with. Or that you may be an experiment that the authorities might misuse.'

Although the basic contradictions in classroom teaching change little over time, there are currently many developments taking place outside the classroom which all the teachers were conscious would affect both the possibilities and limitations of their work. They are the outcome of what has been called 'The Great Debate' on education. It was sparked off in 1976 by a speech by Callaghan, raising doubts about the effectiveness of the education system in producing young people suited for employment in industry and commerce. It developed into a conflict between 'progressives' who wanted to defend their professional autonomy and ideas about educating people for life, and 'reactionaries' who

were concerned to change the education system so as to be more
directly geared to education for jobs. 'There has been a fundamental
shift since then. What is called "the new settlement" in education
involves a much greater centralisation of power, more control over
the curriculum and, on the other hand, notions of participation by
parents and "community". What seems to be happening is the end
of the old consensus. The reformism of the Labour Party and the
professionalism of the teachers and the rise of an academic sociology
of education – the influence of all that is on the wane. It is giving
way to the combination of corporate management and "participation".' That is a familiar combination – as will become apparent
in Chapter 4.

As Patrick put it, 'The move is towards pulling the reins
tighter, more supervision and control from the centre. And that is
something that as teachers we must resist. The thing is – in doing so
we must disentangle what resistance is really in the interests of the
working class, and what is merely professional self-defence. Because
there is an engrained kind of professionalism among teachers that
sees the community and parents, as well as the educational policy
makers, as a threat.'

Not that, for socialists, the introduction of more parent
participation (the other aspect of the new deal) would be without its
contradictions. 'Active parents are often quite reactionary. The
minute you start opening up any kind of debate with parents what
you get is their anxiety about what the school is doing for their
children. That is the way the school has been presented to them.'
Parents often too easily seemed to accept competitive educational
values that socialist teachers may already have rejected. 'The first
thing black parents say on contact with teachers is "What can you
do to help our children stop 'under-achieving' like it says in the
newspapers?" They don't question the way achievement is
measured.' 'So we can't call simplistically for throwing the school
open to the parents,' Patrick said. 'There is going to be a long and
painful period of negotiating. One thing that makes it slower is the
way we as classroom teachers are kept away from the parents. In my
school the parents have to go first to the Head, who knows nothing
at all about the problem.'

Although the teachers saw these dangers in 'parent and
community participation', they also saw new possibilities. The
Great Debate had at least put the question on the agenda: to whom

should teachers be accountable? And it had opened up the opportunity for teachers to challenge the way their work is currently geared to preparing students for a labour market which means dead-end jobs for the vast majority.

The teachers felt strongly that they had to engage with the struggle about the wider issues in education which, although going on outside of the classroom, will directly affect what it is possible to do in it. At the same time they felt strongly that there was a need for collective organisation and mutual support around what happens *inside* the classroom. In this respect they were disappointed with the union, the National Union of Teachers. 'The NUT won't talk about what happens in class. There is no forum in the NUT to talk about what teachers are actually doing.'

Community health council workers

A Community Health Council is a peculiar 'participatory' body, half in and half out of the National Health Service. Its brief is to 'represent the interests of the public in the health service'. We talked to Joan and Kate, two paid workers in an inner city Community Health Council, one of whom is its secretary. They were emphatic that, although the CHC is supposed to be an expression of public opinion, it can only be understood by looking closely at the National Health Service management system, in which it appears to play a necessary part.

The creation of CHCs was part of the new wave of 'participatory' bodies and processes which proliferated in the early 1970s. During the period of restructuring of the National Health Service, around 1973, there were pressures among the various bodies making policy for the service, on the one hand for tighter and more centralised control, and on the other for a formal measure of public participation.

Under the new management system, the local governing bodies of the health service, responsible for the hospitals and for general practice, are Area Health Authorities. They are not elected bodies. They have members appointed to them by various interested official bodies. Above them are Regional Health Authorities and the Department of Health and Social Security. Within the reformed management system itself, there is a process of 'consensus management' whereby the top of each profession share in corporate decision-making. This is accompanied by a complex procedure of consultation within the system.

The 'participatory' part of the mechanism, the point at which 'the public' are brought in, is the Community Health Council, of which there is one to each Health District, with up to thirty members. Half are appointed by the local authorities whose territory the Health District covers. These may, but need not, be councillors. Of the rest, a third are appointed by the Regional Health Authority and two-thirds are named by the voluntary service and community organisations of the area.

The contradictory nature of the CHC lies in the fact that it does offer a politically useful opportunity to organise and voice working-class opinion on health matters. But it also continually tends to involve the working class in legitimating NHS policy as decided above. Joan and Kate had both taken their posts fully conscious of this ambiguity.

The immediate problem they say they face is a stream of requests for help from distressed individuals. 'We don't call ourselves an advice centre, but such a lot of people come in. People with illnesses the NHS can't cure, people with complaints about doctors, people desperate for a second opinion. They think you have the key to unlock the door. They sometimes get angry when you say it can't be done. It's the worst part of the whole job. Our policy is to deal thoroughly with everything that comes through the door – but not to advertise. We believe that would be fraudulent, because there is so little that can be done. It is not productive to deal with individual cases. We have decided it is better to work with campaigning groups.'

One anomaly arising from the inadequacy of the NHS means that these CHC workers, though socialists, sometimes find themselves suggesting to people that they seek help from the private sector of medicine, from osteopaths, acupuncturists or dentists (for crowning work, for instance).

A second demand on the CHC staff and members' time is the process of official consultation. 'The Authority can put things on your agenda. You have to wade through documents coming from them. More than likely they involve proposals for expenditure cuts, hospital closures and so on. If we oppose any of their proposals we are required to put forward alternatives within three months. But we are just not qualified to answer documents in their terms, it would be a very big job for us. They have spent years on them, and we have to do it in a short time. Besides, we are lay people without specialist knowledge.'

Another complaint of the CHC workers is that, in spite of their semi-official position and the flood of planning documents they receive, they lack access to information. They are not allowed direct contact with lower-ranking personnel in the NHS. 'Mr. J, our District Administrator, says we must get it from him. He gets two letters a day from me and must get fed up answering them. He claims not to know what documents to send us. "You'll be flooded with paper" he says. Our trouble is that we can't easily get what we want unless we know precisely how it is drawn up, what document to ask for.' Nor can the CHC workers easily obtain information by observation. They are never supposed to visit hospitals independently. They (and CHC members) are taken on official visits to hospitals, 'formal inspection trips where you have the managers trailing you round'.

One factor above all others, however, seemed to the CHC workers to hem them in. This was the fact that by being expected to be concerned only with the health *service*, the CHC was effectively prevented from ever focusing on the causes of ill health itself. 'Many people come to us with environmental health problems, housing problems, the responsibility of the local authority. But we have no remit to deal with the local council. It is monstrous. We cannot comment on housing – let alone on work, or industry. Yet one thing we feel sure of is that it is capitalism that is damaging people's health.' The statistics show that working-class people are less well than people in higher class groups. 'But no connection is ever made between illness, class and stress.'

The problems that come in through the door of the CHC seem to indicate that ill-health occurs more through the way society is organised than through the patient's own fault, or due to some law of nature. 'Yet the state is telling people to cure themselves. It started this jogging craze. They brought out the "Eating for Health" thing, telling us to eat less fat and sugar. They say nothing about the fact that they promote the consumption of butter by state subsidies. And that most processed food, like baby food, has enormous quantities of sugar in it. They put the blame continually on the victim.'

Joan and Kate felt that it was crucial for the CHC to reject the notion that it should only be concerned with the NHS. As Kate said, 'To avoid perpetuating the illusion that there's nothing that can be done about the causes of ill-health, it's really important that the CHC should be seen to be concerned with what is making us ill. *Health* as well as health care.'

This particular CHC have decided, as have many others, that their most politically productive role is not casework or collaboration with the management, but campaigning. They emphasise however that these struggles are of three kinds. They are about the social causes of ill-health, from 'health and safety' in a local factory, to lead levels on the by-pass. They are against cuts and hospital closures, and for a better-resourced NHS. But they are also about improving people's *experience* of health care. 'We need to fight hospital closures because we need hospital beds and equipment and facilities in this area. And because when hospitals close the burden of care is put back on women in the family. And families in this area just can't cope any more. But, as the women's movement has pointed out so clearly, we should not blind ourselves to the fact that the hospitals, as they are, are authoritarian. They afford us no control over our own health. They are inadequate. And people know it. It is because they don't really feel it is "their" National Health Service that there has been so little organised resistance to the cuts.'

The difficulty for the CHC however is finding a satisfactory model of responsibility and relationship to the local working class. First, it can't be assumed that all members of the CHC itself are going to agree about the campaigning role. Energy and effort goes into negotiating that agreement. Second, it is a question of forming links with unions and community groups. But these are often impermanent, and many of their ideal components are missing: the unions and community groups have not traditionally become involved in questions of health and health care (except those relating to health and safety at work). These have been seen as private matters for the individual or the family. So, it seems to be an unequal struggle between a well-organised hierarchy and a disorganised and fragmented working class.

'It is so hard to confront doctors' power, because it's exercised in situations when you are really on your own and feeling at your most vulnerable. We haven't found any way to do this yet. Even fighting the cuts is difficult because again the people most affected, women caring for relatives at home, are the ones least likely to be in a position to fight back. Anyway, they would feel emotionally very peculiar about saying "Well, actually what I want is for my old mum to be put in a geriatric hospital". With these kinds of situation, developing a coherent socialist strategy seems too much. It isn't on. We do try to keep on *raising* these kinds of issue, though, even if we don't see any clear ways of organising round them, in the hope that things will become clearer in time.'

Even on more commonplace issues, however, like fighting closures, there is no real working-class movement. 'We got every single working-class "organ" in our district to support a campaign against a hospital closure: tenants associations, the trades council, the Labour Party, pensioners, women's groups. But when it came to a demo, these groups, who on paper represent thousands of people, could only mobilise about point-nought-one per cent of them. The only organisation round here with any really active mass base is the methodist church. The minister puts the leaflets in the hymn books and there is always an excellent turn out from there.'

Like the Advice Centre workers, Kate and Joan feel that in the absence of mass working-class support, they have to rely for any feeling of legitimacy they may have on rigorous analysis of their situation and on the fact that at least they are involved in daily practice and contact with many people.

Despite the many constraints which Joan and Kate describe, some CHCs have in fact posed a threat to the orderly working of the NHS management. Some have mobilised thousands of people in resistance to hospital closures. As a result the trend in the DHSS now is to define the position of CHC more precisely, and in particular to involve them more in forward planning for the service. 'Ennals has said, in effect, "Sorry I had to close hospitals against your wishes. These plans were formulated before CHCs were invented. You don't appreciate our reasons. What I am going to do is argue for you to be more closely involved in the planning procedure in future."'

This may seem to offer the CHC earlier warning and more information. But it is also asking the Council to organise the working class to participate in its own deprivation. 'They want us to help them decide what to cut. He is really saying "You will have a chance to endorse hospital closures earlier in future".' And not everybody may recognise the trap. 'The danger for us is that some of

our members, people who really like being on important committees, will lap this up. They may forget to be a body in *opposition* to
AHA policies.'

In the Labour Party

Many socialists who are convinced that electoral democratic
processes are inadequate for bringing about a transition to
socialism, nonetheless join the Labour Party and seek election,
particularly to local councils. This 'Labour left' is important to
other socialists who, however critical they may be of the Labour
Party, know they benefit from the fact that occasionally Labour
leftists are able to secure corners of government for relatively
progressive policies and, at the worst, keep out the right – in the
shape of Tories or the nationalist parties.

An example of the constructive effect of the existence of a
progressive Labour council on other struggles in an area occurs in
the interview with the Advice Centre workers. Labour councils
helped them into existence, and when, subsequently, Conservative
majorities took over the councils the Advice Centres' scope for
political action was seriously curtailed. Yet the Labour left are often
criticised by those socialists who prefer to remain outside the party
and outside electoral systems, for having chosen to wear the familiar
shabby garment of authority, to engage in broken promises and the
management of poverty. In failing, like all contemporary ad-
ministrations are bound to fail, to find solutions to the ravages
caused by capitalism, the Labour left are felt to bring socialism itself
into popular disrepute by meddling with policy.

We talked to three Labour Party activists, two of whom had
recently been elected as councillors in an area with a strong left-
wing council leadership. We asked them about the possibilities and
limitations of their position.

The local authority to which the councillors were elected is in
an inner-city area where there is a particularly high level of
dependence on the state for jobs and services. Housing conditions
there are poor. For most people a council flat in a tower block is
about the best you can hope for. The big firms have disappeared in
search of higher profits elsewhere. So wages are low, whether you
work for the council (now the biggest employer round there) or for
one of the cleaning firms that service the big office blocks that

dominate the landscape. Often you can't get a job at all. The pressure of living and working in such conditions are reflected in the high crime, vandalism and truancy rates and the high level of police activity. For the thirty per cent of the area's population who are black, racism compounds these everyday problems.

All three Labour activists felt strongly that by being in, or close to, power, they had achieved a situation that could be milked for practical advantage to the working class. It had been possible, for instance, to give funding to certain radical community groups and projects; to work with squatting groups over the use of empty housing; to appoint race relations advisers to purge the council bureaucracy of racist practices – in their housing allocation among other things. It had even proved possible for a while to hold down council housing rents.

But they were also uneasily aware of the limitations of their position. 'Whatever we are doing at the moment is within this capitalist framework, anything you do will contain reformist and perhaps reactionary elements. No matter what. Therefore you get into the debate about what is "most progressive", or something like that. It is a debate worth having, but it is not desperately fundamental somehow.' Worse, the councillors were aware of having opted to manage the unmanageable. 'The reality is the budget.' Needs in this poor area were incalculable, resources strictly deficient. 'In Social Services we have been given one-sixth of the funding needed for our three-year plan. And that plan itself would only have begun to touch the problems in our area.' They are in the invidious position, for example, of making policy for a particular day nursery, scheduled to close on account of high lead pollution in the air surrounding its playground. There is no money to relocate it. Should they support its fight to stay open? Is a poisonous nursery better than no nursery?

The limitations on resources posed by central government, and resistance to local rate rises, meant that what they seemed to have taken on was the job of prioritising, choosing what not to fund. 'Social Services committee would have to turn round to the "under-fives campaign", and say "Okay, here is our plan. Given our financial constraints, we cannot build you a nursery without cutting back on some other part of the plan. What do you suggest?"'

In this kind of situation, leftist councillors were finding it difficult to avoid the trap of thinking as a manager, thinking about 'limiting demand'. 'In housing, one councillor was taken on and he's got a revolutionary background and rhetoric. But now even he's talking the language of "you can't put a quart into a pint pot", and "we've got to think about priorities".' Whatever your intentions, resisting the language of management may prove impossible. The problem for the councillors we talked to was to find a new way of thinking and struggling, one that resists taking the management standpoint.

Normally, our class instincts are strongest when it comes to worker/boss relationships. What happens to a Labour group, however left, when it wins an election is that it steps right into the shoes of a boss. 'You see, the biggest employer in the area is us. And the way we as a council relate to our workforce is through very traditional management/worker channels. Before the election we promised to set up a Working Party on Industrial Democracy, to look at council labour relations. After the election nothing was done on our side about it, until we were prompted by the union reps, on the Joint Works Committee. It was embarrassing, really, that it was left to them to raise it, after all we had said beforehand.' And although they kept their promise on that, it has proved difficult in practice for the councillors to link up with their employees on a basis of 'we're on your side'.

The councillors were uneasily recognising that they had not found a way of transforming the boss/worker relationship. 'I think we are, after all, out to get as much as we can for our money, to get the best services possible. We are not for allowing every worker in the town hall to take four days a week holiday just because we've got a left-wing council.'

The other major contradiction lay in the Council's relation with local people. There appeared to be a genuine debate within the Labour Group on the Council as to what the nature of the relationship should be. Some felt that devolution and participation shouldn't go too far. 'Councillors should still be in control.' This was a minority view however. Another minority wanted more involvement with community groups. For instance, they proposed tenant liaison officers to link the tenants' associations closer to the Council. But a majority of the Labour Group turned this down, because they felt that 'that was the opposite of what we should be doing'. It would be an attempt to manage conflict and contain it. It was rejected for that very reason. Yet this same perceptive group was planning 'devolution of services and ward consultation as one of the means by which we can get through to people locally'. Just what could the relationship be between socialist urban managers and a local working class? Was there any option between one of outright emnity, on the one hand, or, on the other, working-class people getting tied up in 'participation' and the managerial logic?

Breaking out of the managerialism of the councillors' role is made particularly difficult because the entire structure of the local authority reinforces a technical rather than a political way of looking at the issues. Key decisions are taken by a Board of Directors, and a sophisticated hierarchy of people with special skills or qualifications ensures their implementation. Senior officers ensure that councillors do not normally have direct access to lower level officers. 'When I went round Management Services I was followed round by the Director', a councillor said, 'and his assistants, and you can imagine going up to some poor worker, trying to talk to him about what he was actually doing, or what he thought about Management Services, when he could be overheard by Mr X, and Mr Y and Mr Z . . .'

The same structure which workers find oppressive to work in, and clients find impossible to penetrate, constrains the councillors: 'We can't get into the Housing Directorate because it is locked to stop angry clients from getting in. It not only keeps them out, it keeps us out too.'

Of course, as with the Advice Centre workers, the councillors were aware that around everything the Council does is the encirclement of the law. 'Everything is governed by statute. You are always caught in any direction you want to go in, really hidebound.' A clear example of this is the relationship of the Council to a group of low-paid women workers in the locality. 'One of the things we have tried to do is put money into workers' co-operatives, and a particularly important one was the women cleaners. They are massively exploited by the companies they work for. So the women cleaners' co-op was set up in the north of the district, with our help and a large low-interest loan. We invited them to tender for council contracts. They put in a tender for cleaning the town hall, worked out the basis of the *lowest rate of pay* that any woman in the Council gets today. And their tender was the highest we received. So the other firms must have been paying even lower wages. And yet we are bound by law to accept the lowest tender. So we ended up supporting the super-exploitative practices of the office-cleaning firms, rather than the workers' co-op.'

'It is central government that makes these rules that govern the activities of local authorities, as it is the government that controls resource allocation. It is central government that stops councils putting up their workers' wages, spending more on improving services, or keeping the rents of council houses down.' The councillors saw this as a stumbling block at every turn. 'If you had a council which was a hundred per cent supportive to class struggle activity going on in the community, and from that perspective was the perfect Council, I think it would still be caught in the same dilemma as we are caught in now.'

They were aware of, and often talked about, the possibility of openly defying central government. But they believed that to engage in such a confrontation might lose them the very thing they had sought election in order to gain, it would involve a breakdown of the services provided by the Council. The knowledge that their action might hurt local people, whether as 'clients' or workers, more than or in addition to hurting the state, they believed was the major barrier to action. 'The Leader says that if we defy central government and go broke locally, the first thing that will happen is that we will not be able to pay the weekly-paid staff, and we will have all the unions against us.'

The thing that above all else heightens the councillors' sense of urgency in finding a course of action is their awareness that if they are trapped, it is a trap that they have entered voluntarily. It is a political role they have chosen to play, not a work situation they are caught up in. There exist few models of appropriate practice for them to draw on. We asked them whether they felt socialists outside the Labour Party had any suggestions about how they might find a way through their managerial predicament. But they felt none of the parties that stay outside the Council wanted to know about the contradictions of going in. 'They don't show their faces. They aren't interested.'

2: **The Predicament**

A number of major predicaments seem to emerge from these conversations. It is not that everyone experiences the state in the same way, but that nearly always a problem experienced by one individual or group is reflected in the experience of others. We discuss below a number of issues that seemed to be recurring in what people told us. The issues are difficult to separate out and pin down for examination, however, because they are interactive. The relation between the state and ourselves is a seamless web.

Resources we need involve us in relations we don't. The major contradiction that seems to arise over and over again in peoples' relation with the state is that the state's institutions offer certain needed goods, benefits or services – things we cannot do without, or would rather have from the state than from any ready alternative source; yet getting these things somehow puts us in an undesirable position. This contradiction takes a number of different forms in our conversations. To win a degree of control over the operations of the local authority, Labour leftists felt they had to fight elections. Yet once elected they found themselves involved in a management situation, employer to low-paid workers. Advice centre workers wanted to obtain legal rights for their 'clients', but to do so they and the people they were helping had to observe the stifling forms of the law, submit to legal procedures, take on the role of plaintiff.

Another expression of this contradiction is found in the interview with teachers. If some socialists and feminists seek higher posts in the educational system they can channel resources to, and defend the interests of, progressive classroom teachers and working-class children. Yet doing this embroils them deeper and deeper, the further up the ladder they go, in hierarchical organisation, in maintaining and observing discipline, in the administration of rules and regulations. It often means accepting the daily practice of sexism and racism too.

An example drawn from an entirely different situation may help to illustrate the way we sometimes have to compromise over *relations* to acquire *resources*. Through the squatting movement, people in need of housing have taken independent, direct action in occupying houses that were standing empty through private and public landlords' inability or unwillingness to administer them. Apart from obtaining somewhere to live, many squatters felt that the act of stepping outside the relations of property, the relation of tenant to landlord, was both challenging to the authorities and encouraging to working-class people. They felt politically good about it. But many local councils responded to squatters by inventing a second-class form of tenure called a 'licence' to occupy short-life housing. They offered licences to people living in squats. It meant semi-security for the squatter, and a renewed grip on housing management for the authority. In most cases a homeless family needed the physical resource of the house for which they were offered a licence so much that they could not consider rejecting it. They submitted to the compromising relationship of landlord and licensee and abandoned the principled political stand of squatting.

Caring helps the (capitalist) world go round. A related but somewhat different point is that as state workers charged with the task of helping people achieve things they need (teachers – O-levels, social workers – extra social security payments, advice centre workers – legal redress), we actively endorse a deceptive illusion. This is the illusion that everyone is equal, with equal rights, freedom of action and access to resources, and that the state can help people achieve this equality. We know from experience that this is untrue. We know that relatively few people can get 'their rights' through the process of law and that the rights which are accessible to them in this way are skimpy. Likewise, we know that relatively few who pass through the education system get O-levels, and that, besides, O-levels are not all that could be wished of a really good education. Yet in present circumstances people really need and want these things, and because of this, we want to help them achieve them. The CHC workers and advice centre workers in our interviews were caught in this contradiction. They were uneasy about the casework they were asked to do because it was so evidently needed, for different reasons, by both the individual and the state. It placed them in a position where to challenge the state's expectations of them as workers, they seemed to be hurting the very people they wanted to help.

In a sense, the social worker or nurse or teacher is in a similar situation at work to that in which she is (and others are) as mother or lover at home. She loves and cares because she is human. But that loving and caring is doubly exploited. It seems to involve her in unpaid and unfair amounts of work in the home. And it causes her to accept underpaid and often heartbreaking work outside. Yet if she resists, she risks hurting herself and those she cares about, merely to ruffle the state a little. Men too are involved in such caring relationships, and sometimes work in caring jobs, and insofar as they do are caught in the same contradiction.

A bed for the night

I hear that in New York
At the corner of 26th Street and Broadway
A man stands every evening during the winter months
And gets beds for the homeless there
By appealing to passers-by.

It won't change the world
It won't improve relations among men
It will not shorten the age of exploitation
But a few men have a bed for the night
For a night the wind is kept from them
The snow meant for them falls on the roadway.

Don't put the book down on reading this, man.

A few people have a bed for the night
For a night the wind is kept from them
The snow meant for them falls on the roadway
But it won't change relations among men
It will not shorten the age of exploitation.

Bertolt Brecht

The imperative of need. Behind this particular contradiction lies the overwhelming problem of actual physical economic need in capitalism. Practical need is so demanding that anyone with any knowhow or resources feels obliged to shove a finger in the dyke. The teachers felt they needed to act as social workers, the advice centre workers as philanthropists and advocates. A strong sense of caring leads first to a liberal and charitable perspective from which it is difficult to move onward to a collective and political one.

Human warmth of feeling presses the individual state worker to respond to the individual client's suffering. Besides, many of these institutions, even the advisory or participatory ones, do have, however limited, some financial resources for such purposes. If they are not used they are wasted. Yet the deployment of them is time consuming. Coping with peoples' needs stops you attacking the source of need. To ignore immediate need and organise a struggle with broader scope, directed against structural evils, seems to be an indulgence, and hard to justify to people who are poor, or sick or homeless. Because in such circumstances they are often reluctant or unable to collectivise their problem and fight in campaigns. If someone comes into the CHC office crippled with arthritis, it is difficult to tell them to join a group to make the NHS change its priorities.

The state workers' problem of choice is rooted in the fact that most people have very little choice. It is difficult for people in tight circumstances to turn a personal tussle with the state into a political struggle against it. Women with children and without collective support can barely get out of the house for a meeting.

Ourselves as wage earners against ourselves as consumers. The indivisible web of our relationship with the state and with each other is such that there seems to exist a conflict between our interests as wage earners working for the state, and our interests as 'clients' of state services, as consumers. Official statements about 'wage/price spirals' warn us off wage demands because of their effect on prices, which take the money out of our pockets as soon as we earn it. The press and other media often seem to play on this theme. And it reflects, although in a distorted way, a real experience for many of the people we talked to.

An example is Maureen's dependence on hospitals, hospital personnel and ambulance services. Her interests are apparently harmed by strikes among these workers. But many hospital workers, especially auxiliary workers, are also women like her, many with children. And they have no recourse, given present union policy, but to strike if they are to get higher wages or better conditions of work, so as to provide for themselves and their families and to continue or improve the service to Maureen.

The conflict between ourselves as wage earners and ourselves as consumers, however, is more apparent than real. What descriptions of the 'wage/price spiral', or of the 'irresponsible public sector worker' leave out of account is the vital third term: capital, which is so often the root of the problem we experience.

Official discourse ignores that there is another party manipulating the situation for gain, or for control. For instance, in official discourse about education, the teacher is often pitted against 'the school child' or 'the parents'. Yet the state has a special interest in the performance of both teacher and child. Somehow this escapes attention. This was clearly expressed in the conversation with John about the experience of being a bus conductor. The conductor is pitted against the passenger in a painful individual way, so that he or she comes to see the struggle as being one to get fewer old age pensioners travelling free on the buses for less of the time, rather than a struggle against the state to get more buses for everybody and more conductors' jobs.

It is not just a problem of consciousness but of practice, however. If, as a state worker, you take militant action of any kind you will run the risk of hurting and angering working-class people more than you hurt the state. Hospital workers, by striking, might gain improvements in wages which would lead to better staffed hospitals. But in taking this course of action they would be likely to alienate the very patients whose strength is needed in this campaign and whom the hospital is conceived as serving. John showed how both individual sabotage of the bus service and union-supported strike action both damaged the service and made even worse the workers' relations with the London working class who use the buses. Militant workers in the state, and their unions, partly because of the contradictions of their situation, partly perhaps because of limited vision blinkered by the way union struggle has developed historically, have difficulty finding forms of action that do not damage the working class as much or more than they damage the state.

Another example of this particular contradiction occurs in the councillors' description of their managerial relationship with their employees. Here the effect is the opposite one. They (stepping into the state role) find themselves saying, in effect, 'We are going to ensure that we exploit *your* labour power to the full, as council workers, in order to give *you*, as members of the public, the best and cheapest possible service.'

So who is defining us and our problems? 'Wage earner' or 'consumer', these categories separate us. It is the state that seems to define who we are. People say, when there is a disagreement about words 'it's only a problem of definition', as though definition is unimportant. But when one group of people have the power to define another group of people, and the authority to make that definition stick, it has real and painful effects.

The main thrust of the Women's Movement has been to overthrow the definition of women imposed on them by men, to define themselves. The struggle of homosexuals is to define their own sexuality in defiance of the limiting definition imposed on them by an aggressively heterosexual culture. In a social world definitions actually construct reality. We tend to act most of the time in the way we have been defined. And the state seems to have a big hand in defining us. It tells us who we are and confuses us about where our interests lie: we are tenants, parents, rate-payers.

The state also seems to represent our problems to us in a way that muddles us as to what is problematic for us and what is problematic for the state. Immigrants who are suffering from racial discrimination, by the state as much as by individual racists, are told they have a 'language problem'.

The Community Health Council workers were frustrated that they were expected to concern themselves only with the NHS, in such a way that it was difficult to talk about the more urgent question of what is making people ill. The teachers were expected to deform their students' learning experience in the interests of examinations, when they know that a pre-ordained number will not even pass them. Exams are really the state's problem, yet they are made to seem the child's. Teaching students to confront this reality was almost a proscribed activity. The advice centre workers were expected to help people in obtaining rehousing in the full knowledge that this would make others have to wait longer for a house. A class problem is posed as an individual one.

It was clear from the interviews that the state's day to day priority is management. Although we are told that the welfare state exists to help us with our problems, it seems to be more concerned with finding ways of dealing with the problem *we are* for the capitalist system. The CHC workers, teachers and advice centre workers all found themselves in the business of managing conflict: channelling dissent about hospital closures through endless con-sultative committees; perpetuating the illusion of equality of opportunity; providing an outlet for people to make complaints without threatening the system.

All along the line, the state uses language and engages in practices that confuse us as to what are problems for the working class and what are problems for the state. Health managers are interested in discharging people from hospital to their homes as soon as possible. They claim this is better for our health and morale. We know it saves them money, however. We are the ones who know best about our real problem (whether our home conditions would help or hinder our recovery). We want the choice. The state workers' predicament is that they often get bogged down in these definitions, especially if they think of themselves as 'neutral professionals'.

The conversation with John, the bus conductor, adds a rider to this. The unions too, are often in the business of redefining our problems and turning them into statements of need that we may go along with, but that we somehow feel do not represent our real requirements. We are led by the union into demanding more overtime rather than better basic pay, more buses, more jobs.

The taboos of sex and class. The workers in the advice centres, the schools and the Community Health Council said they found it very difficult indeed to use class as an explanation, or to propose certain class-based forms of action, even when this seemed to them as socialists to be the most realistic thing to do. Instead, they found themselves speaking of 'parents', 'patients', 'individuals', the public, and 'local people' not only when they really meant to point up these characteristics and attributes, but as an alternative to speaking about 'the working class'. Many are aware that they do this for a quite specific reason. People are designated this way within the terms of reference of the state workers' job, people are grouped into such categories which then become the sphere of the worker's job. Their political actions only have legitimacy if they stick within these terms of reference. To speak of class is to 'break cover'. As long as we act on the false definitions we are all right. When we hit on the correct way of looking at problems, when we have a sense of sex and race and class, we're in trouble.

Advice centre workers address people as individuals (though as we have seen, they would prefer not to) because their legitimacy derives from being caseworkers. The 'public' implies a societal rather than a class interest – hence the Community Health Council's brief is 'to represent the interests of *the public* in the NHS'.

Geography also sometimes has to act as a surrogate for class. The CHC workers felt that they had to look for 'causes of ill-health in the borough', though they were actually aware that more causes of ill-health to the people of the borough lay in industrial practices and employment patterns that are not even national, but international.

State workers are also sometimes shy of invoking class because of the ambiguity they feel in their own class position – as educated, 'professional' people. And because some people who are objectively working class do not identify as such and say 'what's that to do with us?'.

To use surrogates for class, however, is not only the result of being duped into being blind to class realities, or being constrained by the remit of our jobs. Many of the effects of capitalism hit us in specific ways that we experience in common with others in similar specific situations. Problems do present themselves to parents of children differently from the way they present themselves to teachers of those same children. Cyclists do experience the roads in a different way to car users. The way into a socialist consciousness is often through such experiences. The challenge is how to transcend these categories, to see and respond to the more fundamental causes of our problems without losing the sense of immediacy and reality that alone can drive people to act.

A further contradiction exists here, however. We have seen that women's subordination, whether as state workers, as clients of the state or as domestic workers, is not only to the state but also (and with a far longer history) to men. The state ignores sex inequalities in the same way that it obscures class inequalities. The teachers in our interview had a struggle to convince the educational hierarchy in the school that there was anything political about the question of how one is addressed, as a woman, and whether there should be an element of choice about it. The state differentiates between women and men but does not acknowledge that there is any inequality implicit in the differentiation. So the category 'woman' is often one that women feel it is politically progressive to invoke, and the taboo on this is experienced as almost as difficult to outface as the taboo on class.

The need for new ways of fighting back

Traditionally, socialists have given themselves only two models for thinking about the state. One perspective is to see increasing state control as steps towards socialism. The other is to see day-to-day struggle with the state as peripheral or even irrelevant, since capital is 'the real enemy'.

The first view told us that nationalisation was a form of socialism. The Conservatives and the Confederation of British Industry are fiercely opposed to nationalisation – and this reinforces a socialist's belief that there 'must be something in it for us'. When the coal pits were nationalised they put up notices: 'Now the property of the National Coal Board, *for the people.*' We really believed that then. We believed that the National Health Service was 'for the people' too. How far away that seems now. People have come to see the state as something else. Because what we get is not quite what we asked of it. In fact people often prefer private social relations. People sometimes make their own (not capitalist, but libertarian) alternatives where they can, just because the state's provision is not only materially inadequate but actually oppressive.

The second view led us to think that to focus working-class struggle on politics, on the state, was a strategic error. For example, in the late sixties when community workers were developing tactics for community organisation, they often felt it misleading to encourage a local community to see 'the town hall' as the main enemy. They really ought to 'let the dog see the rabbit': capital was the real enemy. Much research was done on ways in which the local council was tied up with local capital. And that was useful – because these connections exist and are little understood. But it was not quite right, or not quite enough. The state (it now appears to us) is 'rabbit' too. It is an important part of the capital relation, in its own right. That the state is important to us, that it plays a big part in our daily lives, that it permeates and deforms our relationships with each other, is clear from the conversations we have reported here. Neither of the traditional socialist ways of understanding the state seem to help deal with the kinds of contradictions people have described to us.

The attack by the Thatcher administration upon certain aspects of the state (council housing, the National Health Service, the Prices Commission) make it urgent to find ways of fighting back that are not simply a defence of something that socialists, along with many working-class people, some of whom vote Conservative, feel is not worthy of our support . . . that in its own way, exploits us. New ways of understanding the state, theorising the state, are needed that match our experience. Perhaps a better theory can help us decide how to go about solving problems of everyday practice as state workers or as people who have a routine relationship with the state in our 'private' lives.

3: **Understanding the Capitalist State**

All the people we talked to experienced the state as contradictory, oppressive, frustrating. Turning to the state for the things we need, or helping others to get what they need may appear to provide an escape route from the injustices of a society based on the pursuit of profit, but there is little sign of this in these conversations. In all of them there is a common thread; the injustice, the inequality, the discrimination of society at large are present too within the state and everything that it does.

Our experience belies the myth of the welfare state

It is common to think of the state as being set apart from the rest of society. People sometimes think of the state as compensating for the inequalities of capitalist society, as redressing the balance between rich and poor. Or, even if the government is clearly not doing much for the poor at present, it is argued that its policies should be changed, that the state 'ought' to help redress the balance more.

This is the dominant, 'Fabian' ideology of the Labour Party. The expansion of the welfare state is identified with the onward march towards socialism. Often people make a distinction between two different sides of the state. They think of the state as having a 'good' (i.e. socialist) side, which would include social services, health, education and nationalised industries; and a 'bad' (i.e. capitalist) side, involving such functions as defence, law and order, and aid to private industry. In this view the struggle for socialism involves trying to expand the good side and restrict the bad side.

The experience of the people we talked to makes it clear that such a view of the state is totally removed from the reality of our everyday contact with it. Maureen's contact with the social worker does not suggest an experience of socialist liberation or even collective solidarity – 'I couldn't have that aggravation again, always being put down and everyone reading your notes'. John described the network of supervision and spying in the state-run buses, and the constant resistance and sabotage of the drivers who feel it is necessary to deliberately let their tyres down and drive slowly. This seems hardly the embryo from which a rational system of socialist transport will grow. Their experience, and the experience of the others we spoke to, stands in stark mockery of the empty abstraction of the Fabian view of the state.

It is true that the welfare state gives us some of the things we need, gives us 'benefits', but it does so in a certain way, in a way that puts us down and oppresses us, in a way that incorporates and perpetuates the inequality and discrimination which run throughout the whole of society. It is not possible to separate off a 'good' side of state activity and see this as being simply in the interests of the working class. As we have seen, even those aspects of state activity which seem most beneficial to the working class are experienced as oppressive by those involved. We receive 'benefits', but somehow the receipt of benefits always confirms that we are underneath, that we are on the receiving end of society, and it is always bound up with submission to supervision and control. And giving us 'benefits' always cuts off the question '*why*'; why do we need the benefits, why are we underneath, why is society unjust and unequal?

The state, then, is not 'our' state. It is 'their' state, an alien, oppressive state.

It is very easy to lose sight of this when the state comes under attack, when the material benefits we receive from the state (including our chances of employment) are being eaten away by the state expenditure cuts introduced by Labour and now increased by the Tories. The immediate reaction of the Left is to fight the cuts, to defend the state. This is very contradictory as we shall argue more fully in the last two chapters, because it implies the state is 'our' state.

An important reason why the cuts have been implemented with such ease, and the reason why the Tories' attacks on the 'overmighty state' have had such popular appeal in the recent election, is precisely that most people experience the state not as 'our' state, but as an oppressive institution. Maureen, for instance, was emphatic that the modern state, despite the resources it offered her, made life worse for her than it was for her mother in Ireland. It is important to realise this if we are to have a realistic basis on which to build a struggle against Tory policies.

A capitalist state in a capitalist society

The state cannot be treated as being totally separate from the society which surrounds it. To understand the state we need to first look at society as a whole.

We live in a class society. We live in a society based on the domination of one class by another, society based on exploitation. The working class produces the wealth but does not control it: it is taken over and controlled by the capitalist class. We can see signs of the class society all around us: in the contrast between rich and poor, in the coexistence of thousands of homeless people and rampant speculation of prestige office blocks, in the 'rationalisations,' which throw thousands of workers on to the rubbish heap of unemployment, in the antagonism which runs through every bit of society.

The exploitation of one class by another is not, of course, peculiar to capitalism. Feudal and slave societies were also based on exploitation. What is peculiar to capitalism is the form which this exploitation takes. The essential characteristic is that under capitalism, the labour power of the worker is bought and sold. It is a commodity. This is different from other class societies. Slave-owners, for example, exploited their slaves by owning them and forcing them to work in return for their keep. Feudal serfs were politically and legally subjected to the rule of their lord and forced to work a certain number of days for the lord. In both of these cases the class nature of the society was fairly obvious, and was recognised by the political and religious institutions.

Under capitalism, however, the relations between the classes are less clear. Society is still based on exploitation: a ruling class still appropriates and controls the wealth produced by the working class. But the worker is not owned by his or her employer, nor is s/he politically and legally inferior to the capitalist. On the contrary, the worker is formally a free and equal citizen, just like the capitalist. The distinction between them is that the latter owns and controls the means of production, whereas the worker has no access to the means of production. S/he therefore has no means of surviving unless s/he enters into a contract of exchange with the capitalist.

In this exchange, the capitalist gives the worker a wage which enables the worker to buy food, clothing, shelter and so on in order to survive. In return the worker gives the capitalist control over his or her labour power for the working day. What the worker produces over and above the value of the wage during that day (the surplus value) belongs to the capitalist. In the same way as the slave-owner appropriates the surplus produced by the slave, and the lord appropriates the surplus produced by the serf, so the capitalist appropriates the surplus produced by the worker. The difference is that under capitalism, exploitation takes place on the basis of formal relations of apparent equality.

In pre-capitalist class societies, class distinctions openly permeated every aspect of social life. Under capitalism, exploitation is concealed under a formal veil, a veil of freedom and equality in exchange. Workers are 'free' to exchange their labour power with any capitalists they choose. This is an 'equal' exchange in the sense that the workers receive the value of their labour power (as defined by the money needed to ensure survival and reproduction). But the 'equal' exchange conceals exploitation, because they do *not* receive the full value of what is produced by their labour power in action.

This does not mean that all workers are fooled by this appearance of freedom and equality into thinking that class exploitation is at an end. Far from it. But it does provide the basis for a whole framework of social forms which protect the status quo by simply denying the existence of class exploitation. Thus, wage negotiations, for example, take as their starting point the formal equality of the exchange relation between worker and capitalist. The slogan 'a fair day's pay for a fair day's work!' assumes this fairness and equality, completely blotting out the relation of exploitation which underlies the contract between worker and 'employer'. And on this basis a whole network of rights and obligations is built up between worker and capitalist, all of which assume that their relation is intrinsically a fair and equal one. The notion of 'unfair dismissal', for example, presupposes that the opposite of dismissal, employment (i.e. exploitation) is 'fair'.

When we say, therefore, that under capitalism, relations of class exploitation 'appear on the surface' as relations between free and equal individuals, we do not mean that everyone is fooled by that appearance. We mean that the way in which workers relate to capitalists (through the sale of their labour power on the market) provides the basis for a host of different structures of social relations which isolate members of classes, and treat them as equal individuals with mutual rights and obligations. Capitalists and workers are treated not only as 'employers and employees' (with the assumption that this is a natural and fair relation), but as 'landlords and tenants', 'manufacturers and consumers', or merged indiscriminately into 'patients', 'passengers', 'voters', 'taxpayers' etc. Society seems to be made up of millions of interconnecting but fundamentally fragmented social relations without any structure. We are confronted by a host of different ways of relating to people, all of which seem to deny the existence of class and class exploitation.

How is the state a capitalist state?

It is common to think of the state as being a capitalist state simply because of *what* it does: defending property against attack, keeping pickets under control, paying subsidies to the monopolies, providing cheap labour power for industry etc. However, the conversations we described in Chapter 1, suggest that, at least as important is *how* the state does things, that is, the social relations embodied in the organisation of the state and its activity. What makes the state a capitalist state is the way in which it is built into the whole structure of capitalist social relations.

Capitalism is a particular system of social relations, of class relations, which appear on the surface as relations between free and equal individuals. The capitalist nature of the state expresses itself in the way that it consolidates those social relations. The categories of the state (that is the categories through which the state deals with people) are built upon the categories of exchange and constitute an extra layer of protective seal over the class relations of capitalist society.

Starting out from the 'free' exchange of commodities (including the labour power of the worker) the whole structure of the political system is built upon equality and citizenship, or upon distinctions which do *not* relate directly to the fundamental antagonism of capitalist production. It treats us as citizens, voters, taxpayers, patients, social security claimants, employers, employees, smokers, non-smokers – on a host of different bases, but *never* on the basis of class, never on a basis which would raise explicitly the question of exploitation and class domination. And so these questions simply get squeezed out of political discussion. *Exploitation is presupposed before bourgeois politics even begin.*

Conflicts within the confines of bourgeois politics concern only the structure of social relations to be built on top of exploitation: the conflicts may be important but they never raise the fundamental question of class exploitation itself. This is the significance of the distinction between politics and economics: to make that distinction a rigid one (as does the whole structure of the bourgeois political system) means that, from the start, you cut yourself off from an understanding of politics as one aspect of the system of relations of production and exploitation.

The state, then, is not just an institution. It is a form of social relations, a class practice. More precisely, it is a process which projects certain forms of organisation upon our everyday activity, forms of organisation which do not pose any threat to the reproduction of capitalist social relations.

When, as at the moment, the development of British capitalism is particularly oppressive (rising unemployment, rising prices, declining social services and so on), the state invites us, not as a class, but *as individuals*, workers and capitalists alike, into the ballot box to mark a cross in the hope that it might influence which party will next try to govern the capitalist system. When capitalism makes us destitute, the state requires us, not to demonstrate as the victims of class domination, but to fill in forms and apply, *as individuals* in need of assistance, for supplementary benefit. When capitalism ruins our health, we are taken as patients into hospitals to be treated as unfortunate *individuals*; the state never assists us to fight back against the *causes* of ill-health. At every step our relation to the state breaks us up, pushes us into certain moulds, removes from sight all mention of class, or exploitation, or anything which might raise the question of the interrelation between our fragmented ills.

Furthermore, the processes by which the state fragments (or confirms the fragmentation of) society at large find their counterpart within the internal organisation of the state apparatus itself. Just as the state deals with people in a fragmented manner as patients, social security claimants, or old age pensioners, so this is reflected in the internal division of labour within the state apparatus between officials who deal with patients, those who deal with social security claimants, those who deal with old age pensioners, and so on.

And just as the receipt of benefits and the definition of the claimant is bound up with a whole network of supervision and control, so within the state a massive system of hierarchical control ensures that the proper division of labour makes it virtually impossible to raise the question of class or exploitation. For a state worker to try to get to the roots of a problem would be to stray beyond the definition of her or his job.

So what is at issue here is not just a question of ideology in a simple sense. It is not just that our minds are constantly bombarded (as indeed they are) with the idea that we are living in a free, democratic society, that illness and poverty are individual problems. It is more than that. Even if we see through all this, even if we see or sense that illness or poverty are problems of society, we are still faced by the problem that any positive action by us seems to require us to jump through certain administrative hoops, to go through certain procedures which, whatever our beliefs, constrain us to act as *individuals* or fragmented groups.

The struggle against the state, therefore, is not just a matter of enlightening people, of showing them that the state is capitalist. It is a problem of trying to develop alternative forms of organisation which will counteract the fragmentation imposed by the state and give material expression to class solidarity. The state is constantly trying to reduce us to abstract individual citizens. We must struggle against that. We must find ways of expressing our struggles *materially* as class struggles.

The two senses of 'state'

How can we use our daily routine contact with the state (as 'clients' or as 'employees') to struggle against the state? This is the problem which cannot be avoided. On the one hand, we have seen that the idea that you can achieve socialism through the state is illusory: the state channels and fragments our struggles in such a way that socialism can never appear on the agenda. On the other hand, to assume that our routine contact with the state cannot be used in the struggle for socialism would be to condemn ourselves to the hopeless dilemma of after-hours socialism. The dilemma of strengthening capitalism by working as agents of the capitalist state during the day and try to weaken it by our socialist activity in the evenings and at weekends. For those of us who work for a state or semi-state body, or who come into routine contact with the state, as claimants, or tenants, or councillors, for instance the question is inescapable: how do we work *in and against* the state?

To talk of working in and against the state implies that we are using the term 'state' in two slightly different senses. So far, we have emphasised the importance of seeing the state not just as an institution, but as a form of social relations, of seeing how the process of state activity takes place. But it is also an institution. Indeed, this is the more common view – to see parliament, the army, judges, as making up a machine, an apparatus, an 'instrument of the ruling class'. When we say we are employed by the state, or that we come into routine contact with the state, we are referring to an institution, a network of hierarchical rules and financial powers and controls. But when we say this, we say as yet nothing about the way in which the state operates.

Therefore we can distinguish between two senses of the word 'state', between the state apparatus, and the state considered as a form or process of social relations. The two senses are closely intertwined, but the distinction is important. The problem of working in and against the state is precisely the problem of turning our routine contact with the state apparatus against the form of social relations which the apparatus is trying to impose upon our actions.

Now, it is very clear that the state apparatus is not neutral. The whole complex of rules, procedures, divisions of competance, the way that buildings are constructed and furniture designed – all seem to press our activities into a certain mould. The teacher slots into a certain hierarchy in the school, s/he is instructed to teach a certain subject during strictly allotted periods of the day, within a classroom in which children are separated from the rest of the world and placed at desks arranged in a neat, orderly pattern. But it cannot be assumed that the form of state workers' activity is inevitably and completely determined by the state apparatus.

We have already seen examples of peoples' contradictory experience of the state, reflecting the contradictions and antagonisms of capitalist society. The process of state activity is continually interrupted by workers' behaviour being inconsistent with the aims of the state apparatus. Teaching is not *always* schooling kids for capitalism, community workers are not *always* acting as 'soft cops'.

In Chapter 6 we shall give examples of this. There is *always* a tendency for a break or disjuncture to exist between the state apparatus and the way it is trying to form our actions. The state apparatus, the network of rules and controls to which we are subject is a fossil, the outcome of past struggles to channel activity into the 'proper' form. As such, it is far from neutral, but it also has a certain hollowness and, if we are strong enough, brittleness. The rules are constantly being resisted and broken: the problem for us is how do we bend and break them in a politically effective way, in a way which would strengthen the struggle for socialism?

The state casts a protective and opaque seal of freedom and equality over the class domination of capitalism, but this is far from being a smooth, impregnable seal. It is more like a thin crust on a seething, bubbling cauldron of soup. Any system based on class exploitation is bound to be unstable, because it is based on conflict, on the oppression of the majority by the minority. Class struggle does not simply erupt on the fringes of capitalism, in occasional surges of militancy. It is there every day, everywhere, in the whole system of antagonistic relations based on the active and daily-repeated exploitation of one class by another.

To think that such a system based on antagonism could ever be stable, could ever be reduced entirely to routine habit, could ever reproduce itself 'normally' without conflict or disruption, as the bourgeoisie would have us believe, is nonsense. We can see all around us that the 'normal' condition of things is one of *instability:* factories, families, schools – all are riven by conflict, disruption and impermanence – far from the havens of peace and tranquility which bourgeois ideology suggests. The veneer of equality and harmony scarcely conceals the daily eruptions of state violence and discrimination on the one hand, and on the other sabotage, truancy, absenteeism, vandalism and the million other acts of rebellion which capital is constantly seeking to control or suppress.

This seething, steaming soup which constantly breaks through the thin crust of bourgeois forms exists inside as well as outside the state apparatus. The antagonisms which constantly disrupt the flow of things outside the state find expression also in direct relation to the state apparatus. Often these antagonisms are expressed simply in individual acts of rebellion with little political consequence, but sometimes they take more significant forms: organisation by claimants, for instance or community workers joining tenants in protests against state housing provision. Everywhere cracks constantly appear in the relation between the state apparatus and the state as a form of capitalist social relations.

4: **Crisis**

The bubbling of the soup is not simply a timeless, continuing process. The whole structure of capitalist social relations (including the state) is inevitably subject to periodic crisis. Crisis is basically a period when the inner contradictions of capitalism make it necessary for the whole structure of class relations to be reorganised. The conflicts which are present all the time become much more intense, the bubbles in the cauldron acquire a new meaning and a new potential. That is why, if we are to have any perspective of change and if we are to be able to relate our own tussles to the general course of class struggle, we must have some idea of how we are situated in relation to the crisis of capitalism.

We know that the state is in upheaval, that the state is in crisis. We know it from the interviews in the first chapter and we know it from our own experience and from what we can see around us. In the last few years the state has taken on the appearance of a battlefield, with cuts in state expenditure, struggles against the cuts, more and more strikes in the public sector, battles against 'scroungers', and sharpening conflicts between state workers and those who try to 'manage' them.

What is this crisis and why should it give us hope? The crisis is not just a crisis of the state but a crisis of capitalist society as a whole. It should give us hope because it shows so clearly what was so pompously and complacently denied throughout the 1950s and early 1960s: that capitalism is inherently unstable.

When we say that we are in the middle of a crisis of capitalism, we do not, unfortunately, mean that capitalism is on the verge of collapse. The last major crisis of world capitalism – in the early 1930s – looked to some as though it might be the final crisis of capitalism. But capitalism survived – it recovered its health, but only through inflicting enormous suffering on the working class, through the horrors of fascism and the slaughter of war.

That crisis (and this) is often referred to as an 'economic crisis'.

The term is misleading, however as the example of the 1930s shows. The crisis has its roots in the immediate relations of production, but its resolution requires the transformation of the whole complex of social relations.

Capitalist development is inevitably subject to crisis. There are times when it is easy for socialists to forget this. During the long period of post-war prosperity (at least it seemed long at the time), it was easy for socialists to accept the prevailing bourgeois wisdom, that Keynesian economic management had put an end to all crises, and that the way forward was through gradual reform. But now all that has changed: the self-satisfied platitudes of the bourgeoisie have been exposed and the crisis-ridden character of capitalism is plain for all to see. The crisis involves an attack on the working class, but it also gives us hope. The system is weak and cannot survive for ever.

Why is crisis inevitable?

Capitalism is an entire social structure based on the exploitation of one class by another. As we have seen, the capitalist class, by virtue of its control of the means of production, is able to compel the working class to work for it, and to take for itself, as profit, the surplus produced by the working class. The capitalist class rules by virtue of its control of capital, of the 'dead labour' of the workers. The means of production already produced by the workers them-selves, are turned against the workers, to exploit them. As Marx put it:

> Capital is dead labour, that, vampire-like only lives by sucking living labour, and lives the more, the more labour it sucks (*Capital* Vol. 1. p.233).

Capitalism is not unstable simply because any system of class domination is bound to be unstable. It is also unstable in another sense. A peculiarity of capital is that it can survive only by exploiting living labour, but its anarchic pursuit of surplus value forces it to drive living labour out of the process of production. In order to exploit their workers more, capitalists replace those workers by machines. Eventually, this leads to a situation in which the amount of surplus value produced by the workers falls in relation to the total amount of capital invested by the capitalists.

In other words, the antagonistic relation between capital and labour, which drives capital unceasingly to increase its exploitation of labour, expresses itself paradoxically in a tendency for the rate of profit to fall. While each individual capital replaces its workers by machinery to maximise its profits, the end result of the unco-ordinated actions of competing capitals is to reduce the general rate of profit. Once profits begin to fall seriously, capitalists start to withdraw their capital from investment, unemployment goes up, wages fall and we have what is seen as a crisis. But the crisis does not simply appear out of the blue: it is merely the clearest expression of the antagonistic relations that are there all the time. The tendency of the rate of profit to fall is merely the economic expression of the social contradictions inherent in capitalist production. Those contradictions periodically become so acute as to interrupt the continuation of that production.

The crisis then is not simply an 'economic' crisis, but a crisis of an entire social structure. It is a crisis which can be resolved for capital only by restructuring those social relations, in such a way that profitable production is allowed to continue. At the most basic level, this drive for profitable production involves increasing the rate of exploitation, the elimination of inefficient businesses through bankruptcy or takeover and with it the destruction of large amounts of capital machinery. But pushing through these changes requires a major transformation of social relations. It involves, at the most basic level, prolonged struggles between capital and labour to get workers to accept new conditions of production, to accept mass redundancies, high unemployment and lower real wages. But this may involve in turn a whole process of negotiation with the trade unions, attempts to integrate the trade union leaders into the state, attempts to control dissent within the unions by means of the reform of industrial relations and so on. It may involve a restructuring of the state's social services as, on the one hand, concessions are given to the trade unions to get them to accept lower wages and redundancies, and, on the other, cuts are made to relieve the burden of taxation on capital. All this involves too a restructuring of family relations, as women are often the first to be made redundant, as the cuts in hospital and other social services throw back caring responsibilities on to the home, where they fall primarily on women as the increased stress and tension at work and out of work take their toll on our 'private' lives.

One need only think of the last major crisis of world capitalism to see that what is at issue goes far beyond the 'economic'. Two major factors contributed to the resolution of that crisis. The first was fascism. Fascism promoted the centralisation of capital, eliminated the less efficient capitals, strengthened the position of national capital on the world market and, above all, greatly increased the rate of exploitation by smashing the working class organisations and holding down wages. There was not, of course, a fascist takeover in all major capitalist countries, but the international movement of capital ensured that after the war all the leading sectors of international capital benefited from the 'achievements' of fascism.

The second major factor which finally brought about the resolution of the crisis of the 1930s was the second world war. This too involved a major defeat for the working class. Not only were millions of workers slaughtered, but everywhere labour was regulated and wages held down. In addition the enormous destruction and depreciation of capital values during the war meant both that demand levels after the war were very much higher and that there was a new basis on which to begin accumulating capital.

The crisis of the 1930s was resolved, then, through a combination of fascism and war. Both of these involved enormous loss and suffering for the working class. But it would be wrong to think of this process in too simplistic a manner for, despite the very major defeats suffered by the working class in the period 1933–45, there were two important features which gave to the pattern of social relations established after the war the character of what many saw as a 'Golden Era'.

These two features were, first, the fact that the victory of the Allies was based on the close incorporation of the working class into the war effort. This involved a whole complex of institutional changes, concessions and promises of further concessions – laying the basis for what is sometimes referred to as 'the post-war settlement'. The second feature was that the unprecedented extent of the defeat of the working class internationally laid the basis for an unprecedented period of capitalist expansion after the war. So working class living standards were allowed to rise. It is in this context that the 'post-war settlement' and the pattern of social and political relations which it installed in Britain has to be understood.

The pattern of relations established after the war is often referred to as Keynesianism. It is the contradictions of this pattern, of Keynesianism, which have now come to the fore in the present crisis.

Keynesianism and the present crisis

When we talk of the present crisis, we are not speaking simply of an 'economic recession', a 'downturn' in the economy which will soon be over, leaving everything as it was before. The crisis is a long drawn-out struggle to restructure the relations between capital and labour. As we have seen, the war established a certain compromise between the classes, a certain *modus vivendi*, or, since the rule of capital was not successfully challenged, what we can call a mode of domination. It is this mode of domination which is now breaking up and being replaced by another. So it is important to try to understand this process.

To some extent, the restructuring of relations between capital and labour has very little to do with the state. It takes place through redundancies, through intensifying the labour process to increase productivity, through inflation and bankruptcies etc. Nevertheless, the role of the state is very important, particularly in the present crisis. This is not because there is any smooth, inevitable trend towards the expansion of the state, but because the nature of the post-war settlement was such that it involved a high degree of state intervention.

As we have seen, the resolution of the last major crisis of capital through fascism and war led to the installation in Britain of a new mode of domination sometimes referred to as 'Keynesianism', based on a commitment to active state involvement in reconciling the conflicts between capital and labour. This involved two things. First, it involved granting material concessions to the working class such as the National Health Service, national insurance, council housing, and aid to industry to maintain employment. All this costs money, but the resolution of the crisis had laid the basis for the rapid expansion of capital internationally, so that the sharp growth in state expenditure was absorbed by capital without too much difficulty.

Secondly, and this was quite inseparable from the first aspect, the increase in state intervention involved a greatly increased role for the state in the reproduction of the social relations of capitalism, in the processing of social conflict into relatively harmless forms. Thus, more and more people were employed by the state. More and more people came into daily routine contact with the state.

What was involved, in Keynesianism then, was not simply the introduction of new policies but a major reorganisation of the way in which bourgeois political relations are shaped, a change in the way in which the working class is officially atomised and regrouped. Of great importance in this reorganisation is the changed role of the trade unions and the growing involvement of trade union leaders in the state's attempt to 'manage' capitalism. But the changed role of the trade unions is merely the core of a more general pattern of government based on trying to meet conflicting demands by incorporating the conflicting interests, by granting limited concessions rather than by seeking an outright confrontation.

The expansion of state expenditure and state activity implied in Keynesian strategy has created a framework in which 'interest groups' could flourish. Relations between these groups and the parts of the state apparatus with which they dealt have become increasingly close. Increasingly, political activity has come to be focused not through parties and parliamentary representatives, but through functionally defined interest groups which maintain direct relations with sections of the bureaucracy. Part of this general development is the tendency for the state apparatus both to deal with people through these pressure groups and to group people together on the basis of functional interests so defined.

Thus, for example, categories such as 'car owners' and 'council house tenants' come, with the expansion of state administration, to play a much more important part in the relations between the state and the classes of society. Also, the state relates to those functionally defined groups through the officially recognised representatives of their interests: the AA and RAC for car-owners, officially recognised tenants' associations for tenants.

A third aspect of the post-war pattern of social relations which is worth underlining is the enormous impact of the 'welfare' services on the way in which the state relates to people. The growth of the welfare state has meant the development of a much more direct relation between the state and members of the 'public'. What is significant is not just the closeness of this relation, but its establishment on an *individual* or, even more important, *family* basis. The welfare services imply recognition that the myth of individual responsibility has lost conviction and that family support structures have been broken down by the force of capitalist development. However it seeks to reinforce our existence as isolated individuals or isolated nuclear family structures, with all the implications for concepts of family responsibility and for the oppression of women that those structures imply.

The Beveridge Report of 1942, the report which officially laid the basis for the creation of the welfare state after the war, was very conscious of the importance of structuring the state action in this area in such a way as to strengthen the family and the position of women in the home. To take just one example:

> The attitude of the housewife to gainful employment outside the home is not and should not be the same as that of the single woman. She has other duties . . . Taken as a whole, the Plan for Social Security puts a premium on marriage in place of penalising it . . . In the next thirty years housewives as Mothers have vital work to do in ensuring the adequate continuance of the British Race and of British ideals in the world (*Beveridge Report*, p. 52).

The family is at the core of the state to an extent that we rarely realise.

What these three examples illustrate is that the emergence of the Keynesian mode of domination involved in many different ways the development of new forms of struggle by the bourgeoisie, of new ways of dividing and atomising the working class. These forms of struggle, these new relations established between capital and labour are not only an indirect response to working class struggle, they also *inevitably* shape that struggle and call forth new forms of organisation, just as inevitably as, in a war, the development of new methods of warfare by one army imposes, willy nilly, new methods upon the other. One consequence of the neglect by marxist theory of the analysis of this historical development of everyday relations between the state and the working class is that there has been little attempt to understand these changes in organisational form.

It is a commonplace to say that Keynesianism is now in crisis. From our perspective, two points are essential in considering this crisis. First, the crisis of Keynesianism is a crisis of capital. Secondly, if we think of Keynesianism not as a set of policies, but as a particular form of dominating, atomising, disarming the working class, then we must not think of the crisis as simply an attack on working class living standards (although this is important). The crisis is also a restructuring of the way in which class conflict is filtered and defined. We need to remember this if we are to develop appropriate ways of combatting the smothering of conflict which keeps capitalism alive.

The crisis dawned in Britain about 1960. During the 1950s the favourable conditions of accumulation established through the experience of fascism and war allowed the apparent reconciliation of conflicting 'interests' by relatively harmonious means and without any major disruption of the established pattern of social relations. From 1960 onwards the clear decline of profitability first in the British and then later in the decade in the world economy made the restructuring of the relations of production increasingly difficult. But at the same time the balance of class forces was such that a radical abandonment of the Keynesian mode of domination was impossible. The result has been a compromise: not a sharp abandonment of the Keynesian mode of domination but its gradual transformation. If originally Keynesianism involved the attempt to reconcile conflicting 'interests' through a combination of institutionalisation and concession, since 1960 the emphasis within this indissoluble combination has been increasingly placed upon institutionalisation with only minimal concession – necessarily so, given the imperatives of capital restructuring.

The compromise reached through this shift in the nature of Keynesianism has not been entirely satisfactory from the point of view of capital. Certainly, massive capital restructuring has taken place. Inefficient firms have gone bankrupt or been taken over by bigger firms: the number of company liquidations more than doubled between 1973 and 1975. The more successful firms have survived by 'rationalising' their workers into unemployment. The number of people unemployed has soared to its highest level since the 1930s. Real wages have been cut back to an unprecedented extent. As *The Economist* put it in September 1977:

The 7 per cent by which the past year's 10 per cent increase in earnings fell behind its 17 per cent increase in prices represents the biggest recorded fall in the average Briton's real disposable

income for over a hundred years: worse than anything that
happened in the 1930s (*The Economist*, 3 September 1977).

The cuts in planned expenditure made in three doses in 1976 were
far greater than any cuts in state expenditure ever made previously.
Women have been pushed back into the family; youth unemployment is worse than ever before; racial tension has grown as blacks
are the first to suffer from the crisis and attempts have been made to
aggravate divisions within the working class.

All this is not negligible. But it is not enough for capital. The
necessity of continuing to appease conflicting interests has prevented restructuring from taking place quickly or radically enough.
Hence the chronic crisis of British capitalism and hence the
continuing pressure for an outright abandonment of the Keynesian
mode of domination.

The transformation of the Keynesian mode of domination has
also involved major changes in the institutional organisation of the
state apparatus, towards what is sometimes called 'corporatism'.
We find it helpful to think of these changes as coming in two phases.
The first phase from the early 1960s onwards saw a considerable
expansion and fragmentation of the state apparatus. The interest
groups (including, first and foremost, the trade unions acting in this
capacity) which had flourished in the climate of expanding state
activity in the 1950s have become increasingly incorporated within
the state apparatus itself, finding an established place on a host of
state bodies, national and local. This has necessarily led to a
fragmentation or disaggregation of the state apparatus itself. This is
expressed, for example, in the enormous growth of semi-state
bodies and 'quangos' at national and local level, often without any
clearly defined relation to central state authority. A second
consequence is the tendency for class conflict to be displaced. What
was formerly expressed as conflict between trade unions and
employers, for example, is now fragmented being expressed partly
in conflicts between representatives and represented (union leaders
and members). Arguably, the end result of this displacement is that
conflict, instead of being more easily controlled, is in fact less easy to
control: hence the instability of the 'corporatist' strategy, so evident
in the last months of the Labour government.

Associated with these institutional changes after 1960 has been
the increasing emphasis on management techniques within the

state apparatus. It seems to us that this development, which has been an integral part of all recent institutional reforms of the state should be seen, not just as part of a general trend towards centralisation but, on the contrary, as counterpart of the general disaggregation of the state apparatus. It results not only from a concern to minimise expenditure and maximise output, and not only from the increased importance of close contact between state and companies, but also from a need to impose uniform patterns of behaviour on an increasingly fragmented state structure. That the development of new techniques of control within the state apparatus has important implications for state workers is obvious.

Challenging capital

However, the institutional changes were not capable of containing the social tensions engendered by the developing crisis. The never-had-it-so-good façade of the fifties began to crack. Anxieties about the rate of growth of public spending and the poor performance of British capital were beginning to be voiced. Strikes again began to disrupt the industrial 'peace' of the post-war period. The significant thing about the struggles of this decade, however, was that they were not limited to trade union or party activity around economic demands, but began to directly challenge capital's *social* relations.

The early sixties saw an outbreak of activity which directly challenged the authority of the law. The Campaign for Nuclear Disarmament must have been one of the biggest campaigns of civil disobedience the western world has ever seen. Later in the decade, protests against the American presence in Vietnam continued to embody this approach to mass action.

As the post war dream of classless garden cities began to fade, the legitimacy of local electoral democracy was put increasingly in question. The wholesale destruction of many inner city areas to make way for tower blocks which people did not want to live in was met with resistance. Tactics included locking councillors into the Council Chamber and lying down in front of bulldozers. Squatters found one partial solution to the housing crisis by occupying empty property. The effect was not only to challenge the way houses were being kept empty while people were homeless, but the idea of private property itself. Squatting also gave many people the physical space to explore collective alternatives to the family, with widespread reverberations. How often have Social Security officers despaired of finding a 'head of household'!

Groups of people who had never come into contact with the labour movement began their own struggles. In 1968 students revolted against the power structure of higher education. They questioned its content and form, rejecting the view that they should passively accept education based on assumptions which reflect the status quo. Often their action involved not only refusing to attend lectures but organising their own collective self-education. Black workers, finding that they had come to Britain to do the lowest paid jobs, also began to resist. They made it clear that they did not want to live in the worst housing and be treated as a scapegoat for the problems caused by capital from unemployment to the 'urban crisis'. Shortly after 'race riots' had marked black people's intention to start fighting back, women began to indicate that an offensive against women's oppression was also in the offing. While women at Fords went on strike for equal pay, women elsewhere were for the first time beginning to assert their right to meet together without men to develop a collective understanding of their oppression.

Industrial struggles also began to take a form which went outside of the traditional forms of struggle of the labour movement, making a far-reaching challenge to capital. Factory closures in the early 1970s met with widespread resistance and a spate of work-ins and occupations. Workers at Upper Clyde Shipbuilders, for instance, took over and ran their own shipyard for nearly a year. Such actions directly confronted the way in which the restructuring of capital takes place at the expense of workers' livelihoods. They were also significant because they asserted that workers have the power and the organisation to take control of their own affairs.

What was important about all these struggles was that in one way or another they not only challenged the economic consequences of capital's exploitation of labour, but the very forms of social organisation which are necessary to maintain this relationship of exploitation.

We see the second phase of institutional change (in the early 1970s) as being associated with the attempt to reassert bourgeois social relations on a more secure basis. The partial failure of the more aggressive strategy pursued by capital in the late 1960s and early 1970s led to a certain regrouping of capital's forces which involved, among other things, a reinforcement of the earlier trends mentioned above and the emergence of two new (and in our view complementary) trends: the development of 'community' as a political category and the strengthening of the repressive apparatus.

Partly in direct response to the unrest of the late 1960s and early 1970s, partly in fear of the possible social consequences of widespread long-term and especially youth unemployment, partly to bolster up the system of representative democracy so obviously bypassed by much of the institutional development in the 1960s, there developed in the early-to-mid 1970s a whole range of new institutions, varying widely from one to another, but all organised around the key concepts of 'community', 'participation', 'direct democracy': community development projects, community health councils, neighbourhood councils, liaison committees with tenants' associations, parent teacher associations, community advice centres, law centres, and planning workshops. The use of a national referendum too is a related development designed to establish a new pattern of relations between the state and the individual, a more direct relation which, like community bodies, bypasses the party as an organisational medium. The ambiguity of the term 'community' (which may refer either to the already organised 'joiners' of society or to an attempt to involve the 'non-joiners') is reflected in that complementary development, the well-documented rise in the overtly repressive strength of the state.

The new attack

The expansion of the state, and especially of the welfare state, since the war has been very much a two-sided process. It has brought material benefits for the working class, but at the same time it has meant a far-reaching penetration of social relations by the state form – it has pushed the oppression and fragmentation implicit in state organisation deep into the texture of society. Over this period (and especially in the last ten years), the state has been remarkably effective in maintaining social stability. At the same time, however, this has been at the cost of delaying the restructuring of social relations which is vital for the future of British capital. And so the pressures have gradually mounted for a radical break with the state-sponsored compromise of the past 35 years.

The outcome of these pressures has been a concerted attack on many of those aspects of the Welfare State which had seemed such a firmly established part of modern capitalism. This attack, begun under the Labour government, is now being pursued with great vigour by the Tories. It involves not just a quantitative reduction in state expenditure but an attack on the whole structure of class compromise and its institutional framework – an attempt to re-shape the links between trade unions and the state, to abandon forms of regional and industrial aid designed to pacify certain parts of the country, to abolish many of the semi-state bodies promoted in the early '70s to foster 'community participation'. Many of the people we spoke to in the earlier section of this pamphlet and many of the positions socialists drifted into in the late '60s and early '70s are particularly vulnerable.

An attack on the capitalist state by the Tories, the most outspoken friends of capitalism? There is nothing paradoxical about that. Their attack on the state has been selective. An administration that gives generous wage increases to army and police cannot be suspected of intending to dismantle the state. Capital is being forced by its own contradictions to reorganise the *way* in which it rules us, to shift from one foot to the other.

But what should our attitude be? Our services and our jobs are being cut or threatened. State workers are at the heart of the class struggle in a way that they have rarely been before. This is reflected in their growing militancy. But how should this widespread anger be directed?

Of course we must defend our jobs and our services. But there is a great danger that in defending ourselves, we will see only one side of the state and forget the other. In our haste to defend our benefits and our jobs, it is easy to lose sight of the oppressive relations in which they enmesh us. In the struggle against the capitalists' attack on the capitalist state, it may seem tactically necessary to paint an unambiguously good picture of the state, to present the Welfare State as a great achievement of the working class, even as a step towards socialism. This is very dangerous. First, because it causes socialism and socialist struggle to fall into understandably bad repute in the working class. Secondly, because it loses an opportunity to pose an alternative to the Labour-Tory, 'more State'/'less State' pendulum, which keeps British capital so secure. Thirdly, because it is unconvincing: people know the state is oppressive and they are not prepared to fight to defend it, as we have seen both in the cuts campaigns and in the recent election.

We must remember that the attack on the state is not only an attack on the working class but also a change in certain forms of domination and control by the ruling class. It involves a slight withdrawal of the tentacles that strangle our struggles and squeeze us into certain shapes. If the expansion of the state was important in ensuring political stability, then it is clear that its contraction involves certain risks for capital. That is what we must try to exploit. Part of exploiting these weaknesses must be the attempt to develop ways of organising which will pose an alternative to the capitalist state. This is what we shall explore in the next two chapters.

5: **Against the State**

In what way can this understanding of the capitalist state help us out of our predicament as socialists within and involved with the state? Can it help us to see and use opportunities for acting as socialists not just after hours but actually within our work or within the moments of our contact with the state?

One or two things can be concluded about struggle. First it is clear that class struggle is not something that happens just at moments when the working class is feeling strong. The theory of capitalism, as we have been discussing it, explains that capital and labour are locked in a structural antagonism, a fundamental relationship of daily exploitation. Our experience, too, tells us that if we don't push back we will be pushed over. So class struggle is an unavoidable, everyday matter. It is not open to choice, it is not some kind of optional extra.

More – this fundamental antagonism does not exist only in industry. It permeates every aspect of our lives including our relationship with the state. Indeed, as we saw, the very existence of the state arises from the necessity to impose and re-impose social relations which deflect class conflict in such a way as to obscure the basic class division in society. It is often hard to recognise as class struggle our many small acts of daily resistance, like getting a relative admitted to hospital, or obtaining an 'exceptional needs' payment. But it is important to remember that it is precisely because the state constitutes us as individuals, patients, parents, families and citizens, pushing us onto ground where almost inevitably we end up fighting back individually, or as ineffectual 'interest groups', that capital is able to impose the social relations which maintain the exploitation of labour.

Nonetheless, we should not get caught in capital's ideological trap. Our daily tussles with the state may appear to be very individualised, but they are essentially a matter of class conflict. Our daily contact with the state is a crucial arena of class struggle.

In the past, however, if as socialists we have concerned ourselves with struggles with the welfare state at all, we have tended to concentrate on questions of resource provision: more and better housing, more hospitals, better teacher-pupil ratios and higher pensions. Increasingly, however, we are coming to realise that it is not enough to fight to keep hospitals open if we do not also challenge the oppressive social relations they embody; that it is insufficient to press for better student-teacher ratios in schools if we do not also challenge what is taught or how it is taught. Socialists involved in struggles over resources are realising that many people choose precisely *not* to give their support to 'fighting the cuts', defending or extending the state apparatus, because they quite reasonably have mixed feelings about the social relations which state institutions embody. What has been missing is conscious struggle against the state as a form of the capital relation.

The theory of the state, as we understand it, shows that there is scope for this. As soon as you abandon the idea of the state merely as an institution, as a function, and begin to recognise it as a form of relations, a whole new way of struggle opens up. It is possible to see many courses of action that can challenge the form of the state's processes while we stay within the state. That is the point: such actions cannot be taken from outside the state, only from within.

More important, it becomes clear that challenge from within is essential. Because the state is a form of relations, its workers and clients, if they do not struggle against it, help to perpetuate it. We are *implicated* in the imposition of capital's social relations. Without oppositional action, we actively perpetuate and recreate a capitalist and sexist and unequal society, not merely by default but through all that we do. We may not make many of the important, top-level decisions or wield any of the serious sanctions. But in a practical day-to-day sense, state workers *are* the state. It only goes forward on our activities. To a lesser extent, all who are in a relationship with the state, cooperating with its services to reproduce labour power and attitudes in the family, are part of the state too.

The fact that we are part of the state, in one way or another, however, gives us a small degree of power for change. This work of cleaning, caring, teaching, representing, moulding cannot be done by computer. Microchips are not enough to sustain and reproduce capital's social relations. This means we can understand and interrupt the process.

To summarise so far:

⋆Class struggle is an unavoidable, everyday matter.
⋆Our daily contact with the state is a crucial arena of class struggle.
⋆It is important to struggle against the state as a form of relations.
⋆Being within the state, we need to oppose the state from within.

So, while we may have no choice at all about being *in* struggle, we do have a choice about how to wage our particular part of it.

There seem to be three main philosophies socialists have about the state, three approaches to everyday decisions that have to be made. One is to get in there and 'use the system for working-class advantage'. People adopting this strategy tend to feel it is ultra-left and unnecessarily negative to turn down opportunities for work and for provision offered by the state. Best to make what we can of a bad job. In this spirit, community workers lead working-class people to take part in local government participation exercises, schooling them in committee procedure and public speaking, in the hope that they can get a fair deal by stating their case through the proper channels.

A second response springs from pessimism. Some socialist state workers say 'it is mere idealism to suppose that as state workers we are anything but state agents'. They feel there is nothing we can do, or should theoretically hope to do, from within our state jobs. Real, pure, working-class struggle can only be waged from outside the state. In this vein, also, people engaged in campaigns may wish to keep state workers well clear of them. 'Keep the council's community workers out of our housing struggle.' Even in their free time and after-hours, state workers may be unwelcome – for instance in some key office in a trades council or a neighbourhood council.

The third common stance towards the state is that of using the law, or state provision, to enable us to carve out a little corner in which we have freedom to organise things in our own way, a non-capitalist way. We may use state-paid salaries or state permission to set up a 'free school' for a small group of children, or a common-ownership housing scheme or workshop. The idea behind this is that we may be able to make a little convivial, socialist clearing in the woods, which can encourage us and be an example to others. This may or may not work – but it is not enough.

Indeed that applies to all three of these ways of thinking. In certain instances all of them can be right. Taken as a whole, they are never enough. As socialists, we have consistently underestimated both the necessity and the possibility of opposing from within.

What kind of struggle?

> 'Socialism is not a fixed, unchanging doctrine. As the world develops, people's insight increases and as new relations come into being, there arise new methods for achieving our goal.'
>
> *Anton Pannekoek*

What do we mean by opposing, or resisting, or challenging the 'state form'? We have seen how the reality of working-class conflict with the state is that it is not simply about fighting over resources, it is also about resisting oppressive social relations, the way that problems capital has created for us are defined as 'our' problems. It is resisting your doctor's insistence that your illness is your fault. It is deflecting the Social Security's attempts to seek a 'head of household', however inappropriate the circumstances. It is rejecting the way racist practices in state institutions become redefined as our 'language problem'. Given the close connection between class and sexual hierarchies, it is also insisting on our right, as women, to choose when and whether we have children; whether to work outside or inside the home; whom to live with. It is, for all of us, defining our sexuality in our own terms.

It is of critical importance, then, that we challenge the state not only as an oppressive apparatus that must be destroyed and replaced in the long run; and not only as an institution which provides us with certain needed services and resources in the short run; but also as a form of relations that has an adverse effect on the way we live today. The state is not like a pane of glass – it can't be smashed in a single blow, once and for all. We are entangled in the web of relations it creates. Our struggle against it must be a continual one, changing shape as the struggle itself, and the state's response to it, create new opportunities.

There are no general rules that we can offer each other about how to choose to wage our struggle, because each situation we experience is different and imposes its own contradictions on us.

Perhaps there are questions we can ask ourselves, however, about each set of circumstances in which we find ourselves:

As state workers we can ask:

★What kind of social relations are involved in our jobs? Is there a hierarchy? Do women and men have different roles? Do people of different races have different roles? Could things be organised differently?

★What kinds of categories of people are we meant to relate to? Individuals? Families? Tenants? Patients? Is this way of thinking about them as a group helpful or confusing? Could we relate to them differently?

★How are the problems we are meant to be solving, sorting out and so on, defined? Who has made the definitions? Are they problems for the working class or for capital? Could the problems be defined differently?

★What do the people we are supposed to relate to really need? Can we help them say it? Do the procedures we are meant to observe help or hinder this expression? Can we avoid them?

★Are we involved in resource management? Keeping people off buses? Out of nurseries? Deciding priorities? How could we do it differently?

★Does what we do help develop autonomy and self-organisation or passivity and dependence? How could we help people struggle from where we are?

As clients of the state, and in our domestic relations we can ask ourselves:

★How is my problem being defined for me? How would I define it for myself? How can I act on my definition?

★How am I expected to behave? How do I want to behave? What costs which I incur for behaving my way? How can they be minimised?

★Who are the other people who experience the same problem as me? Who is implicated in causing me a problem? Who can give me support in defending my choice? Can I offer them anything?

The answers to these questions that we ask ourselves and each other may help us to understand our role as bearers of capital's social relations and give us a lead to action, helping us to see more clearly the choices we have to make.

Material counter-organisation

> 'We don't set one organisation against another, but
> rather one type of organisation against another type
> . . . You don't oppose the bourgeoisie by imitating
> its organisational schemata.'
> *Daniel Cohn-Bendit and Jean-Pierre Duteuil for the March
> 22nd Movement, in* The Student Revolt, *Panther, 1968.*

Asking questions and coming to understand our role as bearers of
capital's social relations is an important activity, but it is not an end
in itself. Challenging the 'state form' does not just involve entering
into arguments about definitions. Our challenge can take place not
just at the level of ideas and argument, but also at a material level
through counter-organisation.

For social workers this may mean not only confronting the idea
that people's inability to manage on a low income is the result of
personal inadequacies, but finding ways to embody this analysis in
practice, for instance by helping 'clients' organise collectively to
challenge the level of benefit they receive, and refusing to give them
individual advice about budgeting. For teachers, it may mean
introducing collective working rather than competition between
students and organising with other teachers and perhaps even with
students and parents too to defend this approach. For health
workers it may mean not just pointing out the links between
capitalist society and ill-health, but fighting for the right to give
assistance to others involved with struggles against the causes of ill-
health (tenants with damp, workers facing a factory hazard) as part
of their NHS work. These actions are *material* because they involve
the concrete provision of skills and resources. They involve *counter-
organisation* in that they challenge bourgeois class practice.

The link between state workers and groups using state
provision can be made most effectively, not by passing motions, but
by action. For state workers this may mean providing concrete
skills, resources or perspectives which assist the struggle of the
'client' groups – *and* being prepared to struggle within our own
context to defend our decision to do this.

The essential point is to find some way of expressing our
particular struggles as class struggles, to struggle in such a way that

our action does not damage other sections of the working class, but rather overcomes the fragmentation of interest which capital tries to impose. It does not simply mean using class rhetoric, joining in mass pickets. Those things are all necessary, but they are insufficient. Material counter-organisation means thinking of our particular struggles as class struggles and trying to find some way to express that in our material organisation.

Much political debate in relation to the state has focused on the problems of making alliances between workers and 'consumers'. Progressives involved in 'community politics' for instance, always advocate writing for support to the Trades Council as the first stage in any campaign. The kinds of counter-organisation that we'll describe below, however, do not involve making institutional links between people involved in different relationships to the state, but rather propose concrete activity which by its nature asserts our common class interests. An important point, too, is that counter-organisation does not mean giving assistance to an abstract class struggle, someone else's struggle. By definition, it is *our* struggle.

As we develop our material forms of struggle we should make sure that they are our own forms, that they do not mirror those of the state and capital. We would like to live in a socialist society, but we cannot yet do so. The least we can do is to organise a socialist struggle, building organisations and practices that prefigure socialism – a socialism free from sexism and racism and other practices in which we oppress each other.

Counter-organisation involves asserting our needs, our definitions. In the context of inescapable daily class antagonism, it means rejecting roles, ways of doing things and definitions which deflect and obscure this conflict. Oppositional action involves acting on our own understanding of class realities. At the same time it also means creating new social relations to replace the deforming ones through which the state contains class struggle. Counter-organisation challenges the traditional boundaries between 'clients' and workers and the non-class categories which we have described. The forms of organisation we have described involve ways of relating to each other which are anti-capitalist and at the same time, in a partial and temporary way, also socialist and feminist: moves towards collective rather than hierarchical ways of working, new relationships between men and women, between adults and children. It is using the ends which we seek as the means of achieving them. This is sometimes called 'prefigurative struggle.'

This approach leads us to reject the kind of political practice which involves thinking entirely in terms of *demands*. While it is important to demand *resources*, one thing we cannot *ask* for is new social relations: we have to make them. Relationships forged in the struggle are not a pleasant by-product of our activities, but an essential part of that struggle. They also let us see what might be possible in a post-capitalist society.

This is also a politics which recognises the need to reintroduce a measure of imagination into our political practice. The analysis in Chapters 3 and 4 explained why so often what we want is not even on the agenda of the state. We want housing that is better than 'adequate' and that meets the needs of all people, not just those of the nuclear family. We want health care which helps us control our own bodies and fight the causes of ill-health; education aimed at encouraging co-operation not competition; a social security system which does not bind women into the family. We know none of these things are possible within a capitalist framework. Yet to limit our action to demands for 'more of the same' is to fail to take the opportunity to challenge capitalism fundamentally by rejecting its agenda, its definitions, its social relations, and thus threaten its stability. It also causes us to miss an opportunity to elaborate for ourselves the kind of social organisation we would like to see.

Relations means sex and race

When you recognise that the struggle you are involved in is against a certain form of relations it becomes clear that anti-sexist and anti-racist actions are an intrinsic part of them. Among the economic demands so often posed by the trade unions, our demands as women or as racial minorities so often seem to be extras tagged on. Now we can see their centrality.

We know that the age-old pattern of unequal relations between men and women has permeated capitalism from top to bottom. The subordination of women is an integral part of the mode of domination that the state is involved in imposing. We have seen how it is implicated by its policies towards the family and women's work, and by the daily practice of its many institutions. So our struggle against sexism and against many aspects of the family that seem to us constraining and deforming is an essential part of the struggle against the 'state form'.

An aspect of the capital relation and the mould which the state tries to impose is challenged every time men and women refuse to define their relations in terms of marriage or try to form continuing alternative types of household. As women in the domestic situation, every time we make an autonomous choice about how we live we are acting politically in relation to the state. The question women face is to understand what the choices are and how to defend them once made. The other side of the coin of women's subordination is the not merely dominant but domineering heterosexuality of the culture we live in, which discriminates so painfully against gay men and women and asexual people.

Again, once we focus on the relational aspect of the state we see racism and imperialism within the capitalist system take on a particular significance. The autonomous struggles of Caribbean or Asian people in Britain, and of Irish Catholics, are in themselves an important challenge to the state.

Now we have identified the kind of predicament we are in, the kind of state we are up against and the kind of struggle we want, we should look at what resources we currently have, what help can be expected from traditional forms of working-class political organis-ation: socialist parties, and the trade unions.

Disappointment in the parties

We have always looked to political parties for ideas about how best to struggle, but it is striking that none of the people we interviewed felt that political parties had anything useful to say about the situation in which they found themselves. They seemed to share the view that neither the social-democratic parties ('the state is on our side and we need more of it') like the Labour Party and increasingly the Communist Party, nor the revolutionary parties ('the state is the enemy and we must smash it') had very much to say about what they should do in their daily practice in relation to the state.

Despite the fact that so many people these days are employed by the state, in particular a very high percentage of socialist militants, both kinds of parties have tended to imply that if you do not work on the factory floor, then political activity must be a matter for evenings and weekends. This does not mean that state workers have been discouraged from activity at the workplace, but that in practice such activity has been confined to trade-union pressure on pay and conditions. This is clearly an important area of struggle, especially for the low paid – it may be more contradictory for some state 'professionals' who already enjoy high salaries and privileged working conditions. But it is not enough. It does nothing to challenge capital's division of our day into 'work' and 'home'. And how do we find the energy to struggle at all if our 'home' worries are never on the agenda?

Ironically, the political parties seem to ignore reality: the politics of work and home. Work is seen only as an economic relation; home is defined as 'private'. At worst they represent our worries about developing a coherent practice in relation to the state as a diversion from more important political tasks. At best, struggles over such matters as how and what to teach in school; what social work is or could be; what domestic relationships are or could be – these things are valued as an added extra.

In many ways, the failure of socialist parties so far to address themselves to our predicament with regard to the state is under-standable in the light of history. The role of the state in class struggle today is not the same as it was in the days when 'classical' marxist theory was developed. The problems of understanding the role of the state in class struggle posed itself rather differently for Lenin, for example. In the society for which he was writing, workers didn't have the same daily round of contacts with the state educational and welfare agencies, nor did the state scrutinise all wage agreements or maintain such close links with their trade unions. The individual socialist's most frequent direct contact with the state agents was likely to be with the most overtly repressive parts of the state apparatus (police and army) and, although this contact was certainly important, it presented no obvious theoretical difficulty.

Moreover, partly because of the limited extent of state intervention, socialist political activity was much more clearly concentrated in the party. Accordingly, Lenin could base his writings on the state upon the assumption that the party existed as a mediating link between the socialist and the state and that, consequently, the only question about the state was the question of the party's strategy against it.

These discussions were, and still are, of great relevance to socialist practice. The injunction to smash the state is as important now as it ever was. But it is not sufficient. It does not adequately tell the socialist in daily contact with the state what smashing the state means, and how s/he can shape her daily activity in such a way that it becomes part of the struggle for socialism. For a teacher in a classroom, the nature of the state is absolutely central, but party strategy will be peripheral to her activity in the classroom unless it addresses the problems she faces there. Or again, take the example of council tenants taking action to compel the local council to eradicate dampness in their houses. Their relation to the local authority will generally be one of direct confrontation. Although individual members of a tenants' group may be members of political parties or groupings, the group's struggles rarely take the form of party struggles (and certainly this is unlikely to be the most effective way of pursuing them).

Besides the limited range of issues to which the parties appear able to address themselves, a further disincentive to many people to joining them is the nature of their internal structure and ways of acting. The narrow conception of 'the political' which tends to exclude 'the personal' from its scope, and which has affected the choice of issues on which to struggle, has often adversely affected internal organisation too. Parties are in the main based on methods of representation in which the leadership gets detached from the base. Often they seem to be insufficiently aware of what is oppressive for women, black people, homosexuals or people with little formal education. This has limited the practical use of the parties to many potential members who feel excluded, subordinated or underestimated within them.

These are some of the reasons, perhaps, why many socialist militants choose not to join a party at all. It is not to say that 'party' is irrelevant. People involved in struggle need others with whom they can develop their ideas, we need mutual support, a class memory. Diffuse, spasmodic and localised activity will not in itself be enough to bring about the fundamental social change that is needed. The parties, though, are contradictory. And in the absence of some major rethinking and restructuring, we are not able to look to political parties for ideas or support in the particular matters explored here: everyday practice in and against the state.

Frustration in the unions

The second traditional channel for class struggle is the trade unions. Many state workers in recent years have become unionised. Public sector union membership has grown dramatically in the last decade. This development is valuable. It has begun to give the lowest paid state worker a new dignity. A black woman hospital worker said to us: 'We used to get treated like dirt, but since the union became more active, they've got to treat us with more respect.' And union membership has helped some state 'professionals' to begin to see themselves as workers, and to see their relation to the working-class movement.

People we interviewed in chapter 1, however, found that joining a union was not a sufficient answer for them. The agenda of most public sector unions is long on pay and conditions, but short on matters concerning the content of the worker's job. Questions like the school examination system, the relationship of workers to patients in hospital, or the complexities of the social work relation, do not take up much time in union meetings. More to the point, public sector union practice seldom if ever challenges the social relations implicit in the state. It doesn't challenge hierarchy, division of labour. Often quite distressing sexist and racist discrimination goes without comment. Many state workers feel that they get little help with a lot of the things that, as socialists, worry them about their job. At worst, unions mirror the contradictions of the state organisations in which they have come into existence.

In the wake of unionisation in the public sector, there has followed a rapid growth of oppositional movements within the unions – such as the National Union of Teachers Rank and File, NALGO Action, and Redder Tape (in the Civil Service). Although very important as a challenge to bureaucratisation in the union they have not provided the answer to our predicament about the state. Their activity often concentrates on producing a more militant version of the union's demands.

The implications of conventional union action in the public sector were highlighted by the winter strikes of 1978–79. These strikes, which involved hospital workers, refuse workers, grave-diggers, school caretakers and others, painfully demonstrated the contradiction between the need to defend the living standards of public sector workers and the immediate consequences of this action for the people who depend on the services these workers provide. It was those who could not afford private treatment who were most distressed by the disruption of the hospitals. It was women, especially working mothers, who were most worried by school caretakers refusing to open school gates and by later action by the NUT in refusing to supervise dinnertime, letting children loose to eat in the chippy and run on the streets.

The leadership of the public sector unions reasoned that pressure put on the people by the interruption of public services becomes, indirectly, pressure put on the state, which will then accede to union demands. But in this way the weakest, already suffering from the mean level of state services, doubly suffer from their withdrawal. Even this strategy is not available to certain groups of state workers, who do not have a ready 'public' to use as their weapon: research workers, for instance, and community workers.

The impact of the winter strikes on the state and on capital was difficult to assess. And newspapers and television stirred up the issues, scapegoating the strikers. But many people not known for their right-wing views commented that they were hurting ordinary people more than the government. It became clear that in future periods of industrial action more imaginative forms of action would have to be developed.

Further, strikes in the public sector have not always been particularly successful in terms of their objectives. We cannot pretend that withdrawing labour has the same effect on the state as on private capital. Precisely because it hurts working-class people more than the state, such action does not impose very effective sanctions on the state. Indeed, a strike in a hospital, for example, may be partially welcomed by management because its tight financial position is eased by not having to pay out wages during the strike. Taking the private sector as a model for action is not appropriate.

Strike action is important for building up confidence in self-organisation, and an ability to struggle further together. It breaks down the isolation imposed in the workplace; the experience of a picket line, blacking movement of goods and services, illustrates dramatically working-class solidarity. And an ability to defend wages and conditions is necessary before any further developments can be expected.

Heralded by the press as a 'wreckers' charter', NUPE's leaflet sets out some new ideas about fighting the cuts aimed specifically at hitting at management.

∗Work to rule and refuse to cooperate with employers who are making cuts.

∗Rearrange work schedules – without discussion with employers – to offset the effects of cuts.

∗Refuse to work with private contractors.

∗Hold meetings, demonstrations or token strikes at times when it will hurt the employers most.

These are just outlines of what can be done. The most effective tactics will depend on the kind of work being done by our members and the nature of the cuts the employer is trying to make.

How it can work

If you are confronted with cuts – get your Union Steward or Branch Secretary to organise a meeting where all of the workers affected can discuss the most effective action. A few examples will show how:

1. The number of town hall cleaners is cut. Members decide to reduce their workload to compensate for the cuts. They agree that the council chamber committee rooms, mayor's parlour and offices of the senior council officials will not be cleaned.

2. A hospital is understaffed because of cuts. Catering staff re-arrange work schedules which make it impossible to provide refreshments for any meetings held at the hospital. Nursing staff insist on adequate cover for wards at all times Porters find it impossible to undertake any jobs other than those strictly laid down in their official duties.

3. Catering staff at town hall hold a token strike which makes it impossible to serve meals to the council members' dining room when the council is meeting.

4. School meals staff, when numbers are reduced or hours cut, refuse to accept extra work or to work faster. The serving of meals is delayed, clearing up is delayed and classes cannot resume on time.

These are just a few examples but they show how NUPE members can force employers to face up to the consequences of any cuts they make.

However, state services, as we have seen, have not developed simply in response to working-class needs and demands. On the contrary, they have as much to do with maintaining the capital relation as with mitigating its harsher consequences. There must therefore be ways in which 'industrial action' can damage the state without disrupting so divisively the provision of needed and useful services to the working class.

The effect of the current policies and practices of the public sector unions has been that many people who are really concerned about their work, who chose it precisely because it was 'worthwhile' work, of use to people, often refuse to join a union. It is not only reactionaries who have been non-militants. People feel 'if you care for people you can't join in with the union'.

The result of the unions' inability to disentangle the contradictions of the state, to recognise that it is the state's resources we need, its relations we don't, has had two harmful effects, therefore. The trade unions are not as big or as strong as they otherwise might be. And 'clients' of state services have not been able to give their wholehearted support to union action.

Autonomous struggles

We saw that (especially in the 1960s) struggles sprang up outside party and union frameworks. We mentioned the Campaign for Nuclear Disarmament, the Women's Movement, the actions of racial minorities and of students. We saw that what was significant about them was that they were not limited, as parties and unions so often are, to negotiating the best terms possible within a totally unacceptable mode of production, but rather that they challenged and confronted capitalist social relations by raising questions that are entirely unresolvable within it. It is no coincidence that, in order to do this, they stepped outside conventional forms of socialist organisation. To oppose relations you need to develop new relations of struggle too.

A second important characteristic of these movements is that they assert that the first step in entering struggle is to understand and act on our own, first-hand experience. This contrasts with the parties, which, drawing their membership from a wide range of people, in many types of situation, offer them a line, and the line is brought to bear in the analysis of each new situation as it develops.

The respect for first-hand experience has, for instance, been an important underpinning of this book. It is reflected in the way we have tried to begin a discussion of theory and tactics with the carefully recorded words of people who are actually involved. Listening to what people have to say and helping others to hear it is the only way to understand capitalist relations. They are essentially personal.

Because it more effectively challenges relations, autonomous struggle can sometimes be more threatening to the state than party and union practices – so often pitched at the level of resources: demands for more pay, or more houses. However, many of the struggles that have gone under the name 'community action' have illustrated the weakness of autonomous organisation. It is based on first-hand experience of bad housing, homelessness, the indignities and impoverishment of 'claiming', the rip-off of supermarket shopping and so on. But too often it has not moved onwards from the sharpness of the personal experience to a realisation of the source of the predicament. Community organisations have often been small and short-lived, competitive and divisive. They have failed to understand the nature of the state and have sometimes been co-opted by the mechanisms the state has produced to integrate them. A consciousness of class was often missing.

Secondly, just as what the party and the union have to offer is so often 'after-hours' activity, attending meetings and distributing leaflets rather than actually transforming the way we do our job from nine till five, so autonomous struggle has often been more a question of consciousness-raising than material counter-organisation.

6: **Oppositional Possibilities Now**

None of the people we talked to in chapter 1 were involved in any particularly dramatic forms of class conflict, yet each was able to identify some space within the conditions of their relationship with the state in which they could resist or challenge the forms of relations imposed on them. Sometimes they suspected the possibility was there but had not known how to use it, or had felt the costs too great or that they did not have sufficient support from others.

From the experience of these people, as well as from our own experience as 'clients' and workers in the state, and from the stories of others we have talked to or read about, we can begin to piece together some examples of oppositional action which illustrate the variety of ways in which the 'state form' encompasses us and ways in which we can begin to resist it.

We realise that these struggles, in themselves are not enough. They are often small, fragmented and isolated. We use them to illustrate possible tactics to challenge the state form of relations, not as an overall strategy for superceding capitalism. They and a growing network of struggles like them are essential, but their significance depends on the extent to which they are integrated into the general struggle for socialism.

Overcoming individualisation. The state tends to individualise us, to diminish our awareness of having a class interest. We can *only* reassert our class identity therefore by collective struggle. Often it is the most productive course of action too.

The teachers we talked to, particularly Mary, had found that when they organised collectively it was possible to give each other support to work in a way which challenged prevailing attitudes in the school. Teachers of different subjects started using their free periods to sit in the classroom for each other's lessons, so that they could discuss problems together afterwards. This was done without the knowledge of the school authorities. The arrangement helped the teachers to develop socialist ideas about their work and to combat the isolation they otherwise felt.

Mary also worked in a department with a number of other socialist teachers. Collective commitment to certain activities like showing films against racism enabled them to widen the scope of what they were able to do. 'Because the whole department decide to do something, there is no way they can stop us doing it.'

Simply to refuse to act individualistically and to insist on collective organisation can be clearly threatening to state institutions that are themselves bureaucratically arranged.

The law centre workers told us: 'We have ten workers. Originally there were official appointments: so many typists, so many receptionists, a book-keeper, a community worker and a number of solicitors. Although we tried to run it collectively even then, the collective discussions were really only about administration, how to give the clients a better service. That was the way the original group had planned it. Now it is different. We have really shared things out more equally. The typists have begun to do the same work as everyone else. Everyone shares the typing and reception work, the chores.

There has been official criticism of this. They think each centre like ours ought to have a director, and there should be a central management committee. Collective running upsets them. They want one person in control so that they can contact that person regularly and make them responsible, sack them if necessary. There has been a whole lot of discussion among the workers about whether we should co-operate in this, do it the way the sponsors want us to. Some of us say "No, we've got to be anarchic, fuck them up every which way we can, so that they take notice that we're here".'

So often, we are asked to compete with each other as individuals or families. Sometimes people see through this trap and find another way of doing things.

Tenants at Sporle Court, an unhealthy block of flats in Battersea, were all hoping for transfers to better estates. With help from the local Peoples Aid and Action Centre, they employed a doctor to interview and examine all the people living there, seventeen families in all. A report resulted which demonstrated that every one of them required rehousing on medical and medico-psychological grounds on account of their housing condition, and they were able to use this in support of their transfer campaign.

Perhaps the private corner into which the state and capital has driven us most relentlessly is in the household of the nuclear family. So it is from there that every little step outwards towards a de-privatising, a social sharing both of functions like dealing with Social Security, but also a spreading of the burdens and rewards of care, can be a challenge not only to 'state form' but to one of the foundations of capitalist organisation.

Rejecting misleading categories. The state habitually addresses us according to categories which, though not entirely false, in that they do reflect an aspect of our real situation, are nonetheless misleading and (as with individualisation) tend to obscure the reality of our identity.

It is impossible altogether to reject these categories, since they refer to part of our experience. But we can in our struggles try to supercede them and act on more widely shared interests. This has often been recognised by people involved in 'community action', who have tried, for instance, to forge working links between council tenants and direct labour building workers, or to bring owner-occupiers and tenants into joint action over housing improvement. Officially-preferred categories so often confuse and set us against each other. Some groups have successfully resisted this divide-and-rule tactic.

One Active Pensioners group, for example, are unusual in defining 'pensioner' as anyone in receipt of a state pension. So as well as elderly people, disabled younger people can be members of their group and their special problems included in campaigns.

The category of 'community' is itself ambiguous. In so far as capitalism tends, with its brusque processes of development, redevelopment and decline, to ignore and trample on people's attempts to forge a sense of belonging, community is something to fight for. But it is a concept often used in official discourse apparently to localise consciousness, to minimise any sense of class, by fomenting rivalry and parochialism.

The Home Office Community Development Project was an interesting example of a state programme, whose intention in this respect was diverted by the workers in it. Many were socialists, and many more became so as a result of what they learned during the course of the project. They were appointed to twelve different local authorities around the country, mainly, though not exclusively, in areas of inner city decline.

They were expected to study and analyse the problems within their respective communities and try to develop community self-help to overcome them. Instead, they rejected the definition of 'community' proposed by the state and its implied boundaries, and compiled joint reports, comparing and analysing on a national level so that the problem of each area came to be seen for what it was – a product not of misfortune or fecklessness, but of capitalism.

Defining ourselves in class terms. The reality that is obscured by individualisation and the misleading categories preferred by the state is that of class. The aim of socialists in the state is therefore to reveal the class nature of society and the state and to find material ways of expressing this class awareness in their struggle.

In 1976 the West Yorkshire Transport Executive announced cuts of £50,000 in the bus budget. This was accepted by the local branch of the T & GWU on assurance that neither jobs nor earnings would be affected. Neither was any initiative to be taken against the cuts by the Leeds Trades Council or political parties.

The Leeds Campaign Against the Cuts approached 'Platform', a small rank-and-file group of bus workers in the city. All agreed that the proposed cuts would affect both bus workers and community. There would be loss of jobs, cuts in take-home pay and that half of the population entirely dependent on public transport would suffer as services deteriorated. It became clear that public transport was an issue on which strong links between workers and consumers were needed. A joint Public Transport Group was set up on which they would work together.

Bus workers found that public protest about inadequate services helped them to put pressure on union officials to consider more militant action against the cuts. They also found that, as they were able to point to inadequate staffing, lack of spare parts for buses, bus users began to understand the connection between government cuts and why 'No Number 86 turned up the other night'. Organising a campaign together they later prevented fare increases of 24 per cent and plan in future to use the tactic of refusal to collect fares, in which they feel the combined class strength of bus workers and users can best be applied.

Especially for 'professional' state workers, to identify the class structure of the conflict is not enough. It is also a question of deciding personally which side you are on in the struggle and making it material by what you do. This has occurred in many different incidents, as when state social workers have reinforced tenants' barricades against state force; or when probation officers have refused to give court reports on squatters.

The class-conscious choice of tactics must surely be extended to strikes in the big public sector manual workers' unions. The tactic of dealing 'only with emergencies' is not always feasible. It is difficult to distinguish emergency cases from routine cases. Everyone in receipt of meals-on-wheels will suffer without them, each one is an emergency. It is because of this that so many state workers in caring jobs, such as home helps, refuse to strike at all. A strategy of continuing to provide resources while refusing to impose the 'state form' on them may be far more threatening to the state than withdrawing labour. It will involve non-cooperation with management, refusal to recognise hierarchies and orders, the introduction of collective decision-making and new kinds of relationship with 'clients'.

Defining our problem our way. The state, as we've seen, tends to define things we experience as a problem in terms which we don't recognise. When we complain, the finger is pointed back at us. We have to insist on defining our problem our way and refusing to shoulder the blame when it rests not with us but with capitalist ways of producing, and capitalist social relations.

How often, when we are ill, we are made to feel guilty. 'I am at risk of lung cancer because I'm addicted to cigarettes; I have liver disease because I can't resist drink.'

Area Health Authorities have a 'health education' budget allocated for teaching the public about self-help, about self-discipline in diet, drink and smoking.

The Community Health Council workers we talked to said 'At first we thought that health education was liberal nonsense. But then we saw that it is possible to use these resources instead for alerting people to the true causes of illnesses and addictions. Through official "health education" it has been possible to explain to people the environmental sources of cancer. They've seen how the stress of work and worry caused by capitalist relations can cause mental illness. And that a lot of over-eating is encouraged by advertising. As a collective activity, identifying the true causes of ill-health is one of the most consciousness-raising things there can be.'

When children regularly refuse to attend school, the education authorities seek the cause and put the blame on the child and the family.

A group of Educational Welfare Officers fought first for the right to have meetings alone, without superiors present, to discuss their work collectively. Out of these meetings and the shared experience of similar problems, they came to understand that truancy is not a problem that arises in the home or in the child, so much as being a problem for the school, created by the school. In doing so they made a choice as to whose side they were on. The next step was to try to develop more appropriate responses to truancy.

In housing, when the council tenant complains to the council of dampness in a flat or house, frequently he or she meets with the response 'It's your own fault.'

Groups of tenants in Glasgow and Edinburgh insisted on rejecting the council's definition of their problem and insisting on their own. In Glasgow they organised a demonstration outside the council's show house on the estate and threatened to open up one of the damp, inhabited houses as an alternative show house. They carried rotting materials into the council chamber. In Edinburgh, where dampness had been prevalent in many council flats, causing sodden walls, fungus and ruined clothing as well as ill-health, the council blamed the lifestyle of the tenants. They instructed them to heat their homes 24 hours a day, seven days a week, and to leave their windows open at the same time. Joint Damp Action Groups formed to bring tenants together from a number of estates. They compared notes with the Glasgow tenants. They tried for three years all the normal procedures of letter writing, lobbying and deputations. Then they organised a mass complain-in, designed to bring the housing maintenance section to a standstill. They occupied the Housing Committee and threatened a rent strike.

In Glasgow and Edinburgh, although they have not yet won the struggle for damp-free houses, these groups have made their definition of the problem stick. Glasgow did award rate rebates, even though they were small ones. Edinburgh has allocated approximately £250,000 to treat damp houses – not enough, but an admission of responsibility.

Stepping outside the brief. The state fragments responsibilities in such a way that different people and different official bodies have the job of dealing with one part and only that part of our problems. Poor housing and poor health are defined and treated as separate problems, even though we know how closely they are related. These divisions of competence mean that the underlying cause of many of our problems, the capitalist social relation, is obscured. We ourselves often fail to see and respond to the problem as a whole. As state workers somehow we have to find ways in our struggle of rejecting these arbitrary divisions and organising in such a way as to bring the totality into view.

CHC workers said: 'We are meant to be attending to the NHS. But we feel there is little to be done about health through the NHS. Health problems arise through low income and poor living conditions and hazardous work. A CHC should say 'Stuff the NHS, we are going to work on questions of health and safety. We believe that exposing and understanding what is making people ill in this community is more important than helping the management to run the NHS.'

They stepped outside their brief, identifying a certain factory as a source of health hazard. A doctor was employed to visit the factory, where the workers were struggling for union recognition. The doctor was asked by the women workers to examine them. She made a report for their use in their struggle, showing the extent among them of skin disease and other illnesses due to working conditions.

Refusing official procedure. By the ritualised practices in which it involves us, the state tends to prevent any direct disruptive expression of our needs. This dampening process seems to be the result of 'representation', of committee procedure, of the formula of 'the right to speak' or to participate, confidentiality. Many productive struggles against the state seem to include a refusal of such state procedures. The process of choosing a representative and giving over to her or him the power to negotiate, excludes the majority from taking a full share in decision-making, and it distances and co-opts the representative.

CHC workers and Council shifted from proper observance of

state procedure to direct action, with good effect. The Area Health Authority announced the closure of a local hospital. 'First we forced the Area Health Authority to consult local people. We had to take them to court over it. But finally, after all the consultation, the Minister did confirm the closure. So we saw that consultation had not worked. The Minister had turned us down. But everyone was angry. We said to ourselves – instead of going through these fruitless procedures of consultation we should make it clear to the AHA just how strongly people feel. We must stop writing letters to the Minister, calling meetings, discussing documents. Instead we will set up a campaign.'

CHC workers contrasted their experience of campaigning with the demoralisation of endless correspondence and negotiation. 'There is so much to be gained by breaking out of the mould. Being on a picket line, on a demonstration gives you a feeling of solidarity, and a better awareness of your own power.'

The experience of many law centre workers of using legal resources offered by the state has led them to conclude that the law, as a promise of equality, is a sham. Besides, the procedures often tie people up and slow them down.

Law centre workers we talked to were advising a group of tenants fighting a redevelopment scheme. Faced with a choice of continuing to play along with the legal process for small returns, or to expose the fraud, they decided the best course of action was to abandon hopes of legal appeal and instead to physically face the bulldozer in passive resistance with the tenants. They chose this course both as a way of dramatising and strengthening working-class action, and exposing the limitations of the view that justice can be secured by legal procedures.

Rejecting managerial priorities. The state is a hierarchy – or more accurately a system of hierarchies. People working in the state often find that there are rules about sticking to the correct level. Councillors are frequently not allowed access to lower officials and vice versa. The contact between councillors and the bureaucracy is often kept to a high level, where it can be controlled. Likewise, in schools, we saw that in some cases the rules prevent classroom teachers having direct contact with parents.

Councillors and people working in the state have sometimes found therefore that an effective challenge to 'state form' and a necessary step in organising is to find material ways of breaking with hierarchical relations, by making contact above and below level, and across departmental boundaries, and to insist on the right to meet without superiors present.

Within the hierarchies, the way to power over decisions is achieved by climbing upward. Social-democratic parties use this ladder to get to the strategic heights from which they hope to influence things in favour of the working class. But we saw earlier how they take on management responsibilities as they climb, and are soon required to abandon the working class, or at best to become unreliable allies. The struggle within and against the state is not a gradualist game using managerial discretion.

The talks we had with backbench Labour councillors and their friends and supporters in the Labour Party, led us to think that there was a clear distinction to be made between oppositional and managerial space. There was a certain amount of useful oppor-tunity-value in being in the Council, but this lay in the chance of dramatising the current situation from a public platform. It was possible (just) to promote or pass resolutions condemning the government's policy of public expenditure cuts, calling on the Council to restore services and defy the government audit. They could make statements about *need*, rather than resources. But they were limited to rhetorical, rather than material struggle in this respect. Because the Council leadership alone had the power to make material decisions – and for them, it seems likely that the one occasion on which they would choose to act oppositionally would be their last.

The backbenchers, recognising its limitations, still felt that their best role was to dramatise the difference between oppositional and managerial priorities in council affairs. Here and there opportunities arose where an oppositional form could be built into council procedure and achieve a certain durability. An example was the appointment of race relations advisers to certain directorates – black officers whose role was to monitor and challenge the normal managerial process.

In the history of local government, a handful of moments stand out as times when the passing of the management buck stopped dead.

In Poplar in 1921, George Lansbury and other councillors refused to accept the instruction of central government to reduce benefit payable to the already starving unemployed. They went to gaol for their decision.

Half a century later, in Clay Cross, Labour councillors, with full support from a working-class area, refused to implement the rent increases imposed under the 1972 Housing Finance Act. They submitted after a long struggle to personal surcharge and were dismissed by the central state and replaced by an appointed Commissioner.

Labour left councillors in the old London borough of St. Pancras in 1956 lowered council rents, had the Whip withdrawn by their own Party and were surcharged personally in the amount of the deficit their action caused in the council books of account.

More recently, the Area Health Authority in Lambeth, Lewisham and Southwark has refused to implement public expenditure cuts in local health service. As a result they have been sacked and the Secretary of State has appointed special Commissioners to make the cuts.

As socialists inside the state, or having a particular concern with the state, we are a long way from knowing clearly what our expectations of elected members on the left should be. What is a left *oppositional* strategy for elected members? Where and when does opposition fade into managerialism? What should be the minimum conditions of our support for social-democratic candidates? If we do not know clearly what we mean by an oppositional strategy and are not ready to give them support in it, we cannot expect elected members to make a class-conscious choice and act oppositionally.

Alternative organisation in struggle. Counter-organisation must be creative. Given some energy and imagination, the way in which our struggle is organised and fought can not only be an opportunity to test and develop socialist ways of doing things, but can in itself challenge capitalist social relations and therefore pose an important threat to the stability of capitalism.

The 'work-in' (as an alternative to the strike, or to accepting redundancies) has been a response to the withdrawal of capital from firms, the closure of factories and public offices. In the public sector, as cuts begin to affect whole units, the kinds of work-in organised at Plaistow, Hounslow, the Elizabeth Garrett Anderson and other hospitals, will become a relevant form of action.

In Hounslow, a 66-bed general hospital was threatened with

closure in 1976. It began a campaign that year. It developed as a work-in during 1977, and the hospital managed to continue in operation until past the closure date. In October, however, the hospital was raided by the authorities in the night, private ambulances hired by the state came and stole away the patients, and beds and furniture were left overturned. After the raid, the hospital was occupied for a further year until the AHA finally agreed to admit to the inadequacies of their current services and the need for a community hospital on the site.

The work-in at the EGA women's hospital started in November 1976, not only keeping the hospital (threatened with closure) open for the use of women, but defending the choice of better social relations within it. Workers and patients asserted the right of women to be treated by women if they so choose, and have attempted to develop alternatives such as the 'Well Woman Clinic' there. Now the Government have agreed to continue to provide some services for women at the hospital.

Common threads

These examples, then, fragmentary and inconclusive as they are, are nonetheless illustrations of *counter-organisation* in opposition to the 'state form'. In their way they are all *oppositional* – they reflect an understanding of the daily experience of disappointment in reformism and gradualism. They are all based on an awareness of *class conflict*, and take class sides. They are *material*, rather than limited to exhortations and resolutions. They are material in another sense too, in that they avoid idealism: they are based on first-hand experience of predicaments, not on the altruistic effort of some politicised people to help others. The struggles described here all *challenge the capital relation* and its *state form*, and they do so by *prefiguring socialist organisation* within the struggle itself, so far as this is possible.

The need for new strategies

As we saw in Chapters 1 and 2, our relationship with the state is always contradictory. We are always liable to lose something. The basic contradiction is that as 'clients' we need the resources the state offers and that in satisfying this need we are necessarily held into the state form of relations. It is no good discussing struggle as though we were fighting from a well-provisioned, well-armed position. It is precisely because we are *not* that we are organising struggle at all. Capital may be in crisis, but often we are in poverty too. So what we can afford to lose will always be limited, and will have to be calculated against what we can hope to gain.

As state workers, we are often in control of material things that other people need, (health care, housing allocations, SS benefits, transport). In choosing how to act to challenge the state we are limited by the hurt we may inflict on other working-class people by doing so. We are limited too, by the fact that we need our jobs, and that any action which poses any real threat to the state will probably lead to attempts to get rid of us.

The balance of choice will not always (or ever) be decided, though, from our individual situation alone. The scope for localised, limited struggles, the extent to which oppositional space can be identified and exploited, depends to a large extent on the balance of class forces more generally. It is different at one historical moment from another, and history is made day by day and week by week, not a century at a time. Our struggles are part of the process of making history and at the same time the form and content of struggles and their degree of success are determined by history. So it is essential that we be aware of what is going on around us, internationally, nationally and in the next department. The same position in the state structure will have different possibilities at different moments in time. An individual's or group's power to bring about change toward socialism does not depend just upon their position and actions, but on the balance of class forces at any given time.

Many marxists, for instance, in the upsurge of the student revolt in Germany in 1968, were swept to the position of professor in universities, where they had the power to develop socialist education. As the socialist tide retreated, people in lesser posts lost their jobs. The professors, with security of tenure, remained, high and dry. They still held the heights but their power to bring about change had been curtailed by the retreat of the struggle around them. So our actions are important for other people too. We may think we are acting on our own behalf, but what we do changes the balance of class forces for others.

The ideas we have developed about struggle within the state have come out of our experience over the last ten years: a decade characterised especially in the first five years by apparently liberal, if contradictory, state initiatives. In the early seventies many of the new developments, from community work to intermediate treatment, were stabs in the dark on the part of the state. These early experiments in new forms of integration and co-option were in many ways fringe initiatives and the abundant oppositional space they offered has been widely documented.

In recent years, as the state has been able to offer less and less by way of concrete resources to the working class to maintain the capital relation, the flood of initiatives reflecting the changed mode of domination has increased and become more main-stream. Learning from its early experiments, the new forms in the state, from devolution and consumer councils to workers' participation in industry and school community managers, are much more sophisticated and highly controlled. Our oppositional opportunities are contracted.

Now we have a Tory government which at the same time as promising unprecedented cuts in welfare spending has increased spending on the state's repressive activities. In this situation, have the things we have learned from the struggles against the state in the last decade any relevance? How appropriate are the ideas we have set out here to the coming period?

One of the first consequences of a Tory electoral victory has been the demise of many 'quangos'. Public expenditure cuts have provided the rationale for an attack on law centres and advice centres. Socialist research will be made more difficult. Pockets of oppositional activity are being threatened as the initiatives that were tried out by the state in the foregoing period are abandoned – the Home Office Community Development Project and community development in other boroughs such as Wandsworth, are examples. In this situation we may have to defend 'participatory' mechanisms however ambiguous they are, if they offer better opportunities for opposition than autocratic and secretive processes of management. There is a new danger in our situation though, that of appearing to endorse, as we struggle for the retention of certain state services, the state itself. We may become caught up in a defence of the 'state form' as well as of state provision. We may find ourselves driven into defending forms of management and decision-making which we rightly feel ambivalent about, just because they are preferable to forms about which we feel even worse.

It seems important that where oppositional space is threatened we seek oppositional ways to defend it wherever we can. A university teacher whose women's studies course comes under attack, for instance, faces a choice. She can write a letter to the professor justifying her activities on the grounds that this is a 'specialist option'. Or she can organise a collective response from students and other teachers asserting their right to be offered the course they want. So often when threatened with cuts or closures we rush to justify ourselves in terms of our usefulness to the state. How often community projects, advice centres or other experimental projects plead 'Don't close us down. We save you money by promoting self-help, we keep people off the streets. We are no trouble really!' And how often has this strategy not only failed but led to demoralisation too.

To defend our activities on the basis that they are wanted and needed by working-class people rather than that they fulfil the state's needs and expectations may seem at first sight much more risky. But we may receive more organised support this way, as well as making our politics – our analysis of the state – very clear through our actions. We must defend the provision we want to have in a way that strengthens rather than undermines the alternative ways of relating to each other and to the state – which we are trying to develop.

It would be a mistake, however, to imagine that Tory rule will mean an end to oppositional space generated by changes in the mode of domination in the earlier period. If the Tory cuts are not to bring about an immediate political crisis, they will have to be accompanied by many more sleights of hand of the variety of the Great Debate in education and the Supplementary Benefit Review. In the coming years, oppositional activity may prove more difficult to organise, but if the Tories carry out their public expenditure plans they may well find themselves in difficulty in continuing to ensure the effective imposition of the 'state form'. Through counter-organisation we may be able to make it even more difficult for them. In altering the mode of domination – decreasing the allocation of resources to 'participatory' and 'community' bodies and increasing it to the police and the armed forces – the Tories are taking a risk. They are shifting weight from one foot to the other, which may mean that we have a chance to catch them off-balance.

An important component of the Tories' ideological attack has been their view that there has been too much state intervention and too much 'socialism'. The popular support in the working class that helped to bring the Tories to power in the 1979 election is built on a profound dislike of the state. People are reasonably angry with the state. They are angry not only at the niggardly nature of its provision but above all at the oppressive and tedious form of relations it involves them in. They place their anger alongside and in alliance with the quite different distaste for these 'welfare' aspects of the state felt by the bourgeoisie. If we as socialists simply defend the state, as provider of services, rather than opposing it for the relations it represents, we will be failing in dialectic as well as failing to respect the good judgment of working-class people based on a wealth of daily experience.

While reactionary, Tory Government policies are also radical. They appear to offer a way out of the stalemate of the last few years. They are explicitly opposed to centralised bureaucracy and state control, both of which the Tories have cleverly associated with 'socialism'. These policies are attractive to working-class people because they speak to their experience of the state.

By contrast, the Labour Party and the labour movement appear to take a much less radical stand, focusing on a defense of the welfare state. Groups to the left of the Labour Party, while pushing for more militant action do not differ fundamentally from this approach. Think of the slogans: 'Save our hospitals', 'Defend jobs and services'. While many labour movement activists have an historic attachment to the welfare state which they see as a major victory, the mass of people are aware that they are not 'our' hospitals or 'our' services. These are not our institutions but *theirs*.

A socialist movement which responds to the Tory attack on the welfare state by taking a defensive stand will not get mass support. Effective socialist opposition to Tory policies must involve helping people grasp what socialist forms of organisation might be like. As we fight back, we need to clearly distinguish what we want from what we have had in the past: the 'socialism' of the welfare state. However horrible Tory policies, people will not join in the struggle unless they feel that they are part of a movement for something different. Wherever there is resistance we need to look for practical ways of giving our struggle a socialist content and a class basis: insisting on our needs, defining things our way, spelling out how we would like it to be.

We recognise that we are arguing for a new approach to socialist politics and that it leaves many urgent questions of political practice still to be answered. What is clear is that if a mass, class-based movement for socialism is to emerge we need new strategies which do not divide us from ourselves and in practical ways embody a socialist vision in opposition to the capitalist state.

Postscript

1: **Living the Crisis**

When the people who feature in Chapter 1 of this book were first telling us about their experience of the state, a Conservative victory at the May 1979 elections seemed imminent but was not yet a fact. Everyone told us then of changes in the way the state relates to people and in the way it requires them to relate to each other, changes they felt had already been occurring for some years. They were sharply apprehensive about future developments heralded by the electoral strength of the Tories.

The return of a Conservative government, led by Margaret Thatcher, has not started us on a *new* trend. Much of what the Tories have done has its beginnings in the period of Jim Callaghan's Labour administration. But ever since the 1979 election we seem to have been impelled into an accelerating vortex of loss, so that the break with the past now appears irreversible.

What do the developments since May 1979 really mean for people? Given the opportunity of writing a postscript to our original thoughts, we went back and talked again to the people we interviewed in Chapter 1. This time we asked them: how is the deepening crisis affecting you; what has a year of Conservative policies meant for you; what effects have these things had on your wellbeing, your job, your relationship with the state?

Everybody we talked to was able to document a perceptible decline in living standards in the last year. Those who are still working in the kind of state agency that has an open door for working class people, the Advice Centre workers and the Community Health Council workers, report that they are under increasing pressure to respond to people's growing needs.

An Advice Centre worker said 'People on supplementary benefit and on pensions are finding it harder now to make ends meet. More homeless people are coming to us for help. There are more fuel debts this year than last.' For Maureen it is clear that her family's cash benefits do not stretch to buy even what they used to.

Her rent and rates have gone up by 20 per cent in six months. Joan, one of the Community Health Council workers, says 'When rent and rates and other kinds of fixed expense go up, people cut back on food. We find pensioners especially are eating less of the essential but expensive foods like fruit, which are basic to health.'

Even higher paid state workers are feeling the cost of inflation and a stagnating wage. 'I feel poorer' Mary said. 'As teachers, Patrick and I are actually earning more than we have ever earned, but we really have to watch what we spend. Things we thought we could just have without calculating, we have to save for now. It is hard to take, that.'

The crisis, and the state's attempts to manage it at the expense of the working class, take a toll in anxiety and stress as well as in terms of money. Maureen's ulcer is troubling her. The health workers painted an alarming picture of increasing mental illness and suicide rates. People's personal relationships seem more subject to strain, especially relations between men and women.

In their contact with the state, people are finding that the resources and facilities available to them are affected. However problematic they felt their relationship with the state to be, they feel the cuts in state services are taking away something they cannot do without, because they do not have an alternative.

Joan and Kate report more hospitals closing down. London Transport has 450 fewer buses on the roads now than this time last year. Queues are longer and so is waiting time, so tempers are even more frayed. Sometimes it is quite little things that together amount to a run down in services and a new meanness in provision. Talking about her school, Mary says 'It is a gradual erosion. If you lose a tape recorder it means you don't get another now. We can't tax and insure the school minibus this year. The school looks tattier than it has ever done, somehow.' Maureen's daughter's school says this is the last year they will have a school holiday-week at the sea. There are to be no second-helpings of school dinners.

An Advice Centre worker told us 'There used to be short-life accommodation that we could direct homeless people to. The Tory Housing Bill means a complete standstill on council housing programmes. They are not acquiring properties, there is less and less we can do.'

The cutback in facilities is combined with a new repressiveness in the terms on which they are offered. An advice worker told us of changes in the nature of social work. 'It's increasingly court work, what they call the "statutory" side of social work. There is much less counselling and support work being done.' Kate told us 'There's a new brutality about in the way people are being treated. The fuel situation is meaning that many people are being cut off for non-payment, especially people with young families. The electricity and gas boards are now much quicker to disconnect supplies. And they have even increased the cost of reconnection. People are living for months at a time without proper heating and lighting, and next winter it is going to get worse.'

People are increasingly insecure about their jobs. The Law Centre workers we met in 1979 are now among 30 similar workers in the one borough who lost their jobs when the Tory council closed all three Centres in the borough. Mary works at teaching part-time now, looking after her own and other children for part of the week. As a result of this domestic commitment her paid job is more at risk. 'I feel my job at school is very much under threat because part-time workers are non-established. We would be the first to go. It is less secure to be a part-timer now than it was a year ago.'

Relations within the state seem to be becoming increasingly unpleasant. The nastiness affects both people in their routine dealings with the state and workers in state jobs. We were told that in London relations between bus conductors and passengers are deteriorating as there are fewer buses on the road, fares are increasing all the time and services often run late.

Mary says that children in her school will soon be packed 35 to a class in place of 30, which will mean a deterioration in the school experience for children and for the teacher. 'There is less money, so the teaching has to be less adventurous. A worse teacher: pupil ratio and less equipment and materials means teaching is becoming more and more a question of crowd control.'

As the cuts, the scrimping and saving, take effect, the work load of many state workers is increased. The incidence of breakdown among bus drivers is high on those routes where one-man buses are in use. 'Headquarters is full of drivers who have had a physical or emotional collapse and have to be redeployed. They say a one-man bus driver can last, in present circumstances, no longer than five years before he has to give up.'

Joan and Kate say that their work at the Community Health Council is intensifying too. 'Consultation documents are coming round about hospital closures all the time. And we have to spend ages trying to find out where less obvious cuts are being made. But what is worse is that we have to put a lot of energy now into fighting to save our own jobs – it is proposed to have fewer CHCs. We're having to find time to resist the loss of our jobs while keeping up the wider struggle about what's happening to the health service.'

As a result of these pressures, many state workers, especially socialists, are demoralised. Are the jobs worth fighting for? Is it even possible to do them?

A teacher said: 'Most reports on reading standards, maths ability and so on, show that they are actually *rising*. But you don't get that impression from the press and TV. Quite the contrary. Teachers are given the idea that they are failing even to teach the three Rs. And so they don't fight. It is difficult to fight for a higher salary if you feel you are not competent anyway.' As the possibilities narrow, socialists who in the past had felt that some of their work could be developed toward a socialist education, now feel more sceptical and cynical about the value of what they are doing. Neil says: 'My generation of teachers, the people who came into it in the early seventies – a lot have left teaching. They were feeling dispirited, having to struggle to defend a system that they themselves felt offered nothing anyway.'

The crisis and its effect on power relations in the world, as well as on immediate realities at home, all create a feeling of anxiety and a narrowing of horizons. 'I feel more fixed on the spot. In the boom there seemed to be infinite possibilities open to me. Now I feel grateful to have a job at all. I am hanging on. I don't feel any more that excitement of thinking where I might go or what I could do next.'

A real fear of the future ran through all the conversations we had. The Bomb is once again on people's minds. They are looking on anxiously as arms spending is raised and our rulers seem to be trying to prepare us psychologically to accept the possibility of war. It becomes almost embarrassing to admit to our own little anxieties in the face of the awfulness of this threat.

In our present situation it is easy to give in to feelings of powerlessness and hopelessness. And we do not wish to under-estimate the extent of the depression and anxiety we all feel. But we think it is important to analyse what is happening to us – to offer tentative understanding, based on the ideas presented in previous chapters, of what capital is trying to do to us and why. Finally, we will look at some of the opportunities offered to us in our new situation. We will examine how despair is turning into anger and resistance, and how opposition to capital could perhaps become the making of socialism.

2: **The New Mode of Domination**

We are living through a new offensive by the ruling class. So much is clear. But seeing that is not enough. If we think of ourselves not just as oppressed but as resisting, as being in struggle, then it is important that we should understand the particular form that the present offensive takes. We need to know what the strengths and weaknesses of capital's attack are, and how it affects our struggle.

History is not a pendulum that swings to and fro between progress and reaction. Each moment of class initiative has a unique contemporary character, moving forward from the one before. We are not witnessing 'a return to the thirties'. The ways in which the ruling class are seeking to weaken us now are sophisticated and experimental. And old responses on our part are no longer appropriate.

In what ways is capital trying to *dis*-organise us? How is it trying to *re*-organise social relations to ensure its own survival? What openings does this reorganisation provide for socialists? What new forms of struggle are being created? What is wrong with our old forms of struggle?

What we need then is not just an analysis that shows that capital is getting tough, that there is more emphasis on repression and less on consent. What we need is to see the changing patterns of rule and the new forms of conflict that are being generated.

It seems to us helpful to think of the changing patterns of rule in terms of a *mode of domination*. What we mean by that phrase is the way in which capital seeks to define, limit and control our resistance to it – the way it attempts to ensure its rule over us. How capital does this affects our lives and our struggles deeply.

As we suggested in Chapter 4, the pattern of rule or mode of domination may be relatively stable over a fairly long period of time. Thus, in Britain, there was a relatively stable pattern of domination – which we referred to as Keynesianism – from the end of the Second World War until the middle of the 1970s. It is essentially crisis which forces capital to seek new ways of imposing its rule.

We have already seen some ways in which the Keynesian mode of domination was becoming less and less satisfactory for capital. The basic strategy of extending the tentacles of the state to strangle class struggle by incorporation and conciliation involved too many risks and too many costs for capital. It was risky, because occasionally capital lost control of the tentacles and found them beginning to turn back against it. (The Home Office Community Development Projects are one example of that.) It was costly, because the conciliation of conflicting interests costs a lot of money, even if the 'concessions' are often miserly: state expenditure was 'getting out of control'. And above all, the need to avoid too many sharp conflicts hindered capital from carrying out the radical restructuring it requires if it is ever to be 'healthy' again.

Some social peace was indeed purchased, but the economy continued to decline. This is not to say that Keynesianism was a failure. On the contrary, the involvement of the labour movement in the Social Contract for instance, was crucially important in defusing the militancy of the early seventies and paving the way for capital's offensive. But the costs involved and above all the increasingly critical decline in the profitability of British capital have now made it necessary for capital to change its tack. The cumulative changes amount to a substantial shift away from the Keynesian mode of domination to something new.

Monetarism

The new mode of domination we refer to as 'monetarism'. To call it 'Thatcherism' would be misleading. It did not arrive with the 1979 election, nor is it transitory or essentially Conservative. Some of the developments we discuss below date back about ten years; most have been at least partially evident since the mid-1970s. The shifts have often been gradual and contradictory. One pattern of domination does not come to replace another overnight. There are always overlaps, combinations, conflicts.

In what follows we try to analyse some aspects of the new mode of domination and how it affects us and our struggles. In this we continue to concentrate on the state. This is not because we see the changes in the state as being the only expression of the new mode of domination. On the contrary, a central part of the new mode of domination is the much more aggressive strategies being pursued by management in private industry. We concentrate on the state because that is the area we know most about, the area in which we have most direct experience. It is important to start out from our own experience if we are to remember the new mode of domination is not just something that is happening to us, an objective process: it is a struggle, of which we are a part.

In our account of the new mode of domination we focus primarily on Britain. But it is important to remember that the crisis is world-wide, even though it clearly takes different forms in different countries, and the thread to a new pattern of domination is evident in many capitalist countries. This trend must be taken very seriously if we recall that it took fascism and war to resolve the last major crisis of capitalism.

In using the expression 'monetarism' we do not mean to imply, as the media do, that it is simply a matter of changes in money policy. The monetarist mode of domination is no more a mere matter of 'economics' than Keynesianism was. Rather it is an attempt to re-organise the way in which class conflict is filtered and defined. It is a bid to find a way out of the crisis for capital. Of course, at one level, monetarism is indeed a set of economic strategies. Keynesianism sought to flatten out the alarming depressive troughs and upward booms of capital's economic cycles. Monetarism rides the waves. Keynesianism's instrument of control is 'management of demand', by changes in the level of taxation and by the use of government spending-power. Monetarism on the contrary invokes monetary discipline and restraint. The government controls the growth in money supply and imposes cash limits on the public authorities in order to reduce the inflation rate. It hopes thereby to encourage productive investment and greater competitiveness in world markets, whilst the abolition of exchange controls and high interest rates on borrowed money ensure no easy shortcuts for domestic industries.

The monetarist strategy reflects a belief that only a recession and rising unemployment can bring down the rate of inflation and prepare the way for wealth-creating enterprise. It incorporates direct material incentives to 'enterprise': tax rates for the rich and for some businesses are sharply cut, and the burden of taxation is shifted from income to expenditure. But there are also incentives of an almost moral kind: above all, management is to be allowed and encouraged to *manage.*

Instead of direct intervention in wage bargaining through 'pay norms', the government exhorts private industry to resist wage claims unless production costs can be reduced by introducing new technology, making workers redundant. Businessmen are promised an end to state meddling with capitalism, through subsidies which help 'lame ducks' i.e. specific firms or industries that are too inefficient to compete. Monetarist theory, producing policies that seek to deepen and prolong the recession, allowing it to take its toll in bankruptcies and unemployment, is a 'bloodletting' cure. No aspirin is offered to damp down the pain.

The response of the capitalists is as nervous as the patient whose blood is being so hopefully but experimentally drained. On the one hand a well-based fear: as the Industry Secretary said in 1979, 'Insolvency is the biggest growth industry in the country.' On the other hand there is an air of excitement and a new bravado – schemes of mutual insurance against strikes; aggressive, coordinated lockouts as in the 1980 printing dispute.

It is important, though, not to think of monetarism simply as a harsh set of economic policies. Questions of economic policy are in any case always questions of class strategy, of how best to organise the exploitation of the working class. In this instance, the shift from Keynesian to monetarist policies is particularly significant because it raises fundamental questions about the role of the state in the reproduction of capitalism. Basically, the monetarists want to reduce the role of the state and to rely more on the market. However, attempting to reduce the role of the state has very wide implications for the way that the state operates and for the patterns of control that capital seeks to impose of us. This is what we must look at more closely now.

'Rolling back the state'

One of the most effective aspects of the Tories' 1979 election campaign was their attack on state bureaucracy. They came to office pledged to cut back drastically on the role that the state plays in our daily lives and to leave more room for free enterprise. Although the Tories have not yet been successful in reducing state employment as much as they hoped, there have been enormous expenditure cuts, particularly on the 'welfare' side of the state. This has involved, among other things, a redefinition and narrowing of the scope of the services provided by the state.

Kate and Joan, the CHC workers told us, 'All pretence of the NHS as a comprehensive service – from the cradle to the grave – has been abandoned.

Its new role is to be an emegency service for those who have not got the resources to get health care privately.' The new housing legislation, too, makes it clear that council house building is to come almost to a halt and that private landlords and owner occupation are to be increasingly privileged. Even the pretence that council housing is a gradually expanding, stable sector of housing for people of many levels of income is to be given up. It is to be a shoddy and hole-riddled safety net for the very poor or those who are deemed inadequate or otherwise problematic.

A useful illustration of this redefinition of state services is higher education. In the 1960s and 1970s, state provision of higher education was based on the 'Robbins principle': all those who wished for it, and had passed the right exams, were entitled to higher education. While in reality the system did discriminate against the working class and against women, it did have some appearance of being comprehensive.

Now, things are changing again. It is not simply a matter of cutting universities, polytechnics and colleges at a time when the number of eighteen-year-olds is expanding, and so of necessity preventing some from getting the chance they would previously have had. Increasingly it is being emphasised that higher education is a privilege, not a right. And the divisions within the system are being made wider.

The Conservative Minister of State, Rhodes Boyson, clearly wishes to see a rigidly differentiated system. At the top, there will be the universities, perhaps shrunk from their present size and with a few notorious troublespots closed down. Students will, he hopes, be thankful to be there, and will forget the radicalism of their predecessors. Then, quite separate, will be the polytechnics and colleges. They will lose their university-like functions of teaching subjects like sociology and pure science. They will be narrowly vocational. They will train middle-grade technicians, who will be kept out of touch with critical, politicising ideas. The most serious conflict within higher education since the Tory victory, at North-

East London Polytechnic, was over an attempt to impose just such a reorganisation.

Redefining the size and scope and function of the 'welfare state' involves shifting the boundary between what is to be seen as public and what is to be seen as private. The new mode of domination will involve the hiving off of some public services to profit-making businesses. This of course is part of monetarist policy: control of the money supply is one side of the coin, the other is standing back to allow a resurgence of market forces.

A transport worker we spoke to pointed to the clause in the current Transport Bill that will enable the licensing of private bus operators to bid for some of London's bus routes. 'It will be the more profitable routes that will go private of course. You won't get a private operator prepared to run buses at eleven at night in lonely areas, carrying drunks and so on. They wouldn't want all of the aggravation and none of the money. So the public bus service will be an even worse disaster than it is now.'

The CHC workers, Joan and Kate, say that the government has introduced a clause in the Health Services Bill to encourage the growth of private medicine, and that it is observably growing fast. 'In our area we have a private GP service operating now, where you pay £50 initially and £5 per visit. The doctors advertise themselves in the papers and are actually using press cuttings describing the Tory cuts and playing on the existence of long waiting lists.' The Health Service is being encouraged to go to the private sector for more of its services such as blood transfusion. 'The difference is that the NHS has to pay for profits as well as service. The result must be either a worse service or exploiting people more.'

In other circumstances, when profits cannot be made, yet the destruction of services cannot politically be afforded, people are to be cajoled into giving their services free. 'Every week the government sends out another press release urging the importance of voluntary helpers in the NHS. Volunteers are being used more by social services in our area too. The local authority have even appointed an assistant home-help organiser to recruit *volunteers* to work alongside paid home helps.'

'Rolling back the state' can never be just a quantitative reduction of state activity. Narrowing the scope of state services, extending the private sphere – all this also involves putting new burdens and worries upon state workers, reorganising relations within the state, reformulating the way in which the state intervenes in our lives and defines our struggles. Partly this is the almost automatic consequence of the expenditure cuts. The cuts in themselves become a means of reimposing discipline and subordination.

The teachers we talked to pointed out that by enforcing economies, by pruning and setting new priorities in schools, the Tories are changing the relations of education just as surely as if they were arguing for new curricula or new rules of discipline. 'They don't need to give a rationale for what they are doing, they are not bothering to spell out an ideology. Just money cuts. Progressive education needs money and when there is a cut the progressive activities are the first to go.' Mary made this quite clear with an example. 'I overheard our headmaster talking to another on the phone. He said "the economic climate will teach these airy-fairy liberal teachers a thing or two. It will have to be talk-and-chalk from now on. They'll learn what real teaching is".'

But there are other more overt ways in which the expenditure cuts are being accompanied by a reformulation of the role of the state and its relation to our struggles. Firstly, the monetarist approach involves a centralisation of the state, a tightening of the ring of those who have access to even a semblance of power, a shift from participation to exclusion. Secondly, there is the development of new ways of disorganising and dividing us. Thirdly, there is a shift to more overt repression.

From incorporation to exclusion

We saw that Keynesianism was a costly strategy. Trying to conciliate conflicting interests by getting them to participate in the management of the country inevitably meant granting some material concessions. Under monetarism, the pursuit of a tight monetary policy involves abandoning this costly strategy of co-option/concession. Consequently, there is a centralisation of the state, a tightening of the relations of power. Fewer interests are 'consulted', fewer have access to the processes of decision-making. Most of all, this affects the trade unions and the other bodies which claimed to represent the working class in the corridors of power. If Keynesianism was based upon the attempt to incorporate the working class into the system of domination, then monetarism is based upon a new strategy of exclusion from the institutions of power. This is not a total turnabout. Some people were always excluded from the Keynesian compromise – think of the nationalist population of Ulster. And even now we are still very far from a complete abandonment of attempts to deal with conflict by absorbing it and smothering it. Nevertheless, we are witnessing the beginnings of a highly significant shift in strategy.

The exclusion of the working class takes many forms. At the most obvious level, it means exclusion from paid work for many as the total of unemployment rises to 2 million or more. It involves a severing of some of the ties that had been constructed between local councils and the local working class. The state is reneging on many of its offers of 'participation' and 'consultation' of the sixties and early seventies. Its earlier enthusiasm for devolution of aspects of the administration, for community organisation to encourage 'joiners', has noticeably waned. And just as the Keynesian process of developing structures of consultation and negotiation between local councils and their 'public' has given way to more arbitrary and exclusive ways of doing things, so the central state is giving less emphasis to the process of consultation and partnership between itself and local councils, taking more direct control.

The proposed new local government legislation affords an example. Political differences do occur at local level through the electoral process. Local Conservative or Labour majorities on councils are able to exercise a modest amount of choice over the raising of cash and allocating of resources. This sometimes makes it difficult for the central state to be sure of being able to effect its policies fully and swiftly. Now that cutting local authority expenditure has become of vital importance to state and capital, some of the old reliance on persuasion and example has to give way to powerful central state sanctions.

As part of its attempt to reduce the Public Sector Borrowing Requirement – the money the state has to borrow to cover the gap between income from taxes and expenditure – the central state has recently imposed dramatic reductions in the Rate Support Grant it administers to local authorities and which makes up more than half their spending. Some authorities, particularly those that are Tory-controlled, have responded by cutting their expenditure on services, in the spirit of the Tory decision. But a few Labour-controlled councils have refused to cut services. Instead of making cuts they are using the autonomy they have at present to increase their other sources of income, raising rates to unprecedented levels. In spite of the fact that this does eventually charge up the cost of the crisis to the working class, it is nonetheless out of line with monetarist policy. It does nothing to reduce spending.

The initial impact of the Conservative policies on the working class has led to an electoral swing back to Labour, which has brought the Labour Party back into office in a number of urban authorities. A small but significant number of these may resist making the required cuts. So the new Local Government Bill seeks to enable central government selectively to punish councils for excessive rate increases. In this and other ways the already limited power of local councils to join in the making of decisions about their income and expenditure will be curtailed. The decisions will be made for them.

The process of exclusion is not confined to the state and people's relations to the state. It is evident as well in industry. The talk aroused by the Bullock Report, of worker participation, of the right of unions to have access to management information – this has given way to the harder language of tough management. The sacking of Derek Robinson of British Leyland (which we discuss further below), the prolonged lockout at *The Times* – these are examples of exclusion of a kind that was hardly thinkable in the days when the notion of 'conciliation' dominated industrial relations.

Of course, the shift from incorporation to exclusion is not always naked. It may suit the ruling class to keep some of the trappings of participation and consultation – so long as these do not fundamentally hinder them in their plans. Many of the institutions characteristic of the Keynesian mode of domination – for example the Price Commission and similar 'quangos' – are simply being closed down. However, in other instances the institutions themselves are being retained, but purposefully restructured, with less emphasis on participation. The Community Health Council workers told us that while they may escape without complete closure, they were being threatened with amalgamation and new terms of reference. 'In finding out and expressing what users of the NHS and lower-paid workers in hospitals really felt about health services, some CHCs stopped being a mere safety valve for discontent. They opposed cuts, criticised professional views of medicine, raised embarrassing questions about the causes of ill-health. What the Tories want is for us to go back purely to processing individual complaints.'

New ways of dividing and disorganising us

The exclusion of the working class from positions of 'influence' creates problems not only for the working class but also for capital. Incorporation into the institutions of the state was one of the key strategies for controlling the working class. Abandoning that strategy involves real dangers for capital, dangers well illustrated by the recent explosion of anger in Bristol. The spontaneous eruption of the St. Paul's district of Bristol in April 1980, in the face of police provocation, dramatically demonstrated the risks to 'order' in the monetarist policy of exclusion and repression. Suddenly the press and media were full of worried capitalist spokespeople saying 'if it can happen in Bristol it can happen anywhere'.

If the strategy of incorporation is no longer to be used so much, then it is clear that there must be increased reliance on other means of control. Of these the most obvious is open repression. But there are much more insidious ways of dividing and disorganising us, which do not always seem to come from the state and which do not always strike us as being political at all. We could probably all tell of new forms of disorganising us which arise in our daily lives. General features which seem particularly important are the increased use of money as a means of control and the new emphasis on the family and especially the particular impact of the new mode of domination on relationships between men and women.

One of the new ways of dividing us is the use of money as a means of control within the state. Of course, money has always been important as a means of control in capitalist society generally. It is money that sets the horizons of our possibilities and dreams. It is in large part the lack of money that forces us out to alienating work or keeps us imprisoned in the home. Capitalist society is a society in which the price that commodities will fetch in the market-place is what matters, not the capacity they have to satisfy real human needs.

The capitalist state has certainly never been immune from the logic of money. Nevertheless, under the Keynesian mode large sectors of state activity were planned in terms of material things; so many hospitals were to be built, so many teachers hired. Growth was planned within programmes – health, housing, education. If on any one of these programmes the cost turned out to be more than anticipated, an authority could go back to the Treasury and ask for more money. This system has been gradually (and now almost entirely) replaced by a system of cash limits. You are given a cash limit of so many £s, and are absolutely forbidden to exceed it. Within the state too, money now rules. The cash limit system is officially presented simply in terms of the 'need' to control public spending and cut the public sector borrowing requirement. But, from the point of view of class domination, cash limits have another, more subtle effect. They dis-organise our struggle by forcing us to fight against each other.

If we are state workers, our employers can (and do) say to us: 'We'll grant your pay claim, but we'll have to make some of you redundant to pay for it.' If we struggle for better nursery facilities, the council can say 'Fine, you can have them, but only if you tell us which old folks home to shut instead.' In the Health Service they can say, 'Yes, a thousand people a year do die because there aren't enough kidney machines. We could save them. But only by ending other forms of care – it's your choice.' What new strategies are needed on the part of socialists working within the state and those who use the services to avoid being thrown off balance by this shift in class relations?

The other most salient feature of the monetarist mode of disorganising resistance is the process whereby situations where we were or could be dealt with as a collective group are progressively changed so that we are dealt with singly or as families. Of course, previous chapters have shown that Keynesianism also does this. It is certainly a mistake to be nostalgic for Keynesianism, harking back to the days when our masters treated us more gently. Capitalism depends for its survival upon individualising us, and the official denial of the class reality experienced by working class people underlay Keynesianism as much as monetarism. Nevertheless, the growth of state intervention under Keynesianism often created at least a basis upon which one could begin to organise collective action – even if the state tried to contain such action within categories that obscured the real problems. Under the new regime, each closure of a nursery, hospital, old peoples' home often means, in the longer term, one opportunity less for any form of collective action. Each closure means pushing back more of our worries into the privacy of the home.

Forcing us back into the family is a way of 'reprivatising' us. As shown in chapter 4, the Keynesian system of class relations depended on a particular relationship between the state and the family. Nevertheless, Keynesianism did, even though in limited and distorted ways, lift some burdens from women in the home. Old people's homes did allow some escape from the exhausting task of caring for aged relatives, although at the cost, in many cases, of unhappiness and guilt. The NHS did remove some of the worry surrounding ill health. However patchily and grudgingly, the state did provide some facilities for contraception and abortion. And many women were escaping from the home, if only to the different slavery of wage work, for part of their day.

It is important then to recognise that monetarism involves not only a restructuring of industry, and of the state, but a *restructuring of the family*. The repeated attacks on abortion will inevitably undermine women's choice and autonomy. But nearly every aspect of the cuts shifts the balance of 'care' back onto the family, deepening the entrapment of women. Many nurseries are to close. Ending school meals, or raising their price, so that children have to bring sandwiches, means one more thing for the mother to think about. 'Community care' instead of psychiatric or geriatric hospitals becomes a euphemism for more unpaid work by women within the family.

In the world of waged work, the trend to an increase in women's employment that we have seen for many years may well be reversed. This is partly because the state is the prime employer of women, and state employment is to be cut. But more significantly, the development of the microprocessor is going to threaten routine assembly jobs and commercial clerical work, the other spheres of women's employment, on an enormous scale.

Men's jobs are often better represented and protected by trade unionism than these characteristic jobs into which women are forced. Many of the more highly skilled and better rewarded occupations have historically been sequestered by men. Engineering and printing are examples. A situation arises where technological innovation is being used by capitalism and the state to divide and rule. All too often men use their union strength to ensure that it is women rather than men whose jobs or earnings are affected first.

One consequence of monetarism forcing us back into the family is that it will be in our private lives, 'invisible from politics', that many of the effects of the crisis will be worked out. Hospital closures do not mean more people dying in the street, they do mean more domestic work and worry. The monetarist gamble is that the miseries of unemployment will be expressed, not in public disorder but in private despair. The anger at falling living standards will be dissipated into worry over housekeeping and numbed by valium. Again, the state and capital are in a position to divide and rule us through the different roles that men and women conventionally play in the management of household finance: both men and women bringing money in (men more than women as a rule); but women primarily taking responsibility for spending, for making ends meet.

Consciously or unconsciously, the monetarist strategy is already playing on that. So the Tories have cut income tax, with the predominant effect of boosting male pay packets, while clawing the revenue back from VAT, which comes mainly from women's housekeeping money. Tensions between men and women will increase because of the crisis and the new class strategy.

We cannot afford to gloss over these ways in which the monetarist mode of domination differentially affects women and men. Monetarism may well reinforce the ways in which men act as agents of capital's domination, through the mechanism of the sexual division of labour at home and at work. But this is not the only way in which the relations between women and men seem to be changing. Men are often the ones who carry the oppressiveness of capitalist relations into the lives of women. But we should not let the class relations of capitalism make us forget that class domination has always been intertwined with the exercise of men's power over women.

The new mode of domination may foster the power of men *as men*. We've shown how women are being shifted out of waged work and back into the home, or trapped within lower-paid jobs, their choice limited by skimped expenditure on contraception research and advice, the tightening of abortion facilities. Such processes can only serve to strengthen men's long-standing ability to dispose of women's labour in the home and to dominate women's sexuality and reproduction.

A widespread response to the crisis and the monetarist policies is an upsurge of violence – both outside and inside the home – as people act out their individual rage. It is not always remembered that this violence is, in practice, overwhelmingly male violence. And not all of it is directed against property, or the state, or even by men against each other. Much of it is borne individually by women.

Clearly we have to resist the tendency of capitalism to divide us yet further, to look for all the common interests that can unite men and women in the struggle for socialism. But there must also be an intensification of the struggle by women against male power.

Repression

The increasing use of open state repression is an inevitable part of that 'freedom' so loved by the Tories. Narrowing the scope of state services and excluding people from any semblance of access to power necessarily leads to new problems of control and to the increasingly open use of force to solve or contain those problems. It is no coincidence that a reduction in welfare expenditure should be accompanied by a rise in expenditure on police and army. The expansion of the overtly repressive arm of the state is one of the best documented aspects of monetarism. The increasingly high profile of both police and army, the important role played by groups such as the SPG and the SAS, the repressive implications of the development of nuclear energy have all been well documented elsewhere.

But the growing emphasis on repression is expressed not only in the increased use of violence by the state and the higher status accorded to the police and army. More than that there is an intensification of surveillance, supervision and repression throughout the whole of the state, which inevitably involves us whether we are state workers or 'clients'.

To some extent the growth of state surveillance is associated with the development of the new technology. The microprocessor enhances capital's possibilities of control in a number of ways. First, the 'strong state' needs to process a vast amount of information if it is reliably to identify its 'subversives' in order to repress them. The microprocessor gives it that potential: fully automated telephone tapping, for example, is almost a technological actuality.

Secondly, microprocessors and electronic equipment offer two distinct kinds of advantages to capital for control over the production process. In industries such as those that involve repetitive assembly work it can dramatically reduce the need for workers. In many cases such jobs are filled by low-paid, relatively unorganised workers – often women – and lay-offs are easy to implement.

In other kinds of industry, where skilled workers' unions have traditionally held tight control over the labour process, the introduction of electronics can be used to challenge that control. The application of computer-aided photocomposition to the printing industry is an example. By reducing the amount of skill needed for the work, by combining some tasks and eliminating others, by blurring the demarcation lines between jobs normally done by different unions, the new systems are ideal tools for capital to destroy union organisation and power, enabling more effective, direct and exploitative management.

These same gains that electronics offer to capitalist employers are attractive also to those who manage the bureaucracies of the civil service and local authorities. A number of government departments and councils are undertaking trials of automated office equipment. An unofficial report on the use of word processors in the council offices in Bradford show what can happen. 'The machines are in constant operation and are programmed by the rate material comes in. The workers have one ten minute break in the morning and afternoon, and otherwise have no contact with other workers during office time. All new work comes in through a special anti-static glass box and no non-section workers enter the room. The operator has almost no contact with the finished product . . . The existing tenuous relationship between a typist and her work is finally broken altogether. There is no sense any longer in which it is her work.'

During the century or more in which machinery has been applied to industrial production to bring the organisation of work under direct control by the manager, the office worker, still using the modest technology of pen and paper, filing cabinet and typewriter, has retained the 'privilege' of slacker discipline and more discretion at work. Now the computer and its adjuncts, the 'electronic office', offer capital the chance of achieving at last the 'real subordination' of office workers, in commerce, industry and within the state.

In the first edition of *In and Against the State* we concentrated on certain kinds of state 'professional' and 'caring' jobs and the contradictions they represented for socialists. If we understand the new mode of domination correctly, we should shortly detect a great deal of conflict about the relations of work of people in clerical and junior administrative posts. The state aims to shed 102,000 civil service jobs in five years. Even if some state functions are abandoned entirely, much of the saving will certainly have to be achieved by increasing the productivity of the state workers that remain. The attempt to routinise and automate these jobs, and to increase direct control over the people in them, is already provoking resistance – and this may well enable socialists in these jobs to place the issue of the nature of their work squarely on the agenda.

Microprocessors have attracted a great deal of attention. Less talked about, but perhaps more insidious are the many other ways in which the climate of austerity leads to more repressive relations between the state and those who deal with it, and within the state apparatus itself.

Thus, for example, the growth of unemployment creates new relations of dependence on the state and new relations of control. Each year, hundreds of thousands more people are signing on as unemployed. This brings them into more direct interaction with the 'welfare' side of state activity – and this offers potential for capitalist control of the working class. The reduction of the real value of benefits that we have seen in recent months is not simply a matter of saving money. It is also quite openly designed to force people to take (and try to keep) whatever boring, low-paid job they are offered. The removal of the 'earnings-related' extra benefit for the newly unemployed is clearly intended to have this effect. And the partial withdrawal of benefits from strikers' families is designed to make workers think more cautiously before considering industrial action. The repression increasingly comes in the shape not of a warning but a retribution: hospital occupations have been dealt with much more summarily, patients and workers being quickly and violently evicted.

Less obvious, but equally important, are the more informal ways of tightening up. The old separation of 'undeserving' from 'deserving' poor never completely vanished under Keynesianism, and is now reappearing openly. The DHSS is more and more ready to threaten to remove benefit from those who do not conform – the 'workshy'. This is indicated in the differential increases in money benefits as well as the massive increase in the degree of DHSS surveillance of allegedly 'fraudulent' claimants.

In other areas of welfare too, monetarist strategy seems to involve renewed emphasis on surveillance to identify and monitor areas of possible unruliness, and on exclusion of 'dangerous' elements. In schools, increasing resort is had to 'sin bins', special units apart from normal education where troublesome children can be subjected to a selective routine. The Tories are creating remand centres to give a 'short, sharp shock' to young offenders. Their punitive military regime is said to be alarming even to those who first advocated such a measure, and making those who are paid to impose it uneasy.

It is very important to think of the growth of state repression not only as something involving them – the police and the army. Whether as state workers or 'clients' it is something that involves *us*, that confronts us with ever sharper problems in our daily lives. If we are teachers, we find that a new importance is being attached to exams and to marking. If we are social workers we find ourselves more closely sucked into the allocation of 'scarce resources'. If we have any sort of responsibility for finance, we find ourselves increasingly faced by 'hard decisions' in ensuring that cash allocations are not overspent – the sort of 'hard decisions' that management has always had to face. Whatever we do we find that avoiding the cuts often involves 'getting results', and that results are usually measured in terms that imply an increase in control and supervision.

As the room for manoeuvre becomes more restricted, it becomes more important than ever that we should think about the political implications of our daily practice, about the relation between our nine-to-five activity and the struggle for socialism. Especially if we are state workers, the changes in our situation mean that we have to examine even more honestly whose side we are acting on. What are the limits of our willingness to fulfil the expectations the state has of us? How can we develop a practice of opposition?

3: Anger, Resistance and the Making of Socialism

The collapse of the Keynesian class strategy has taken with it our last little illusions about the chance of a reformed and tolerable capitalism. We can see more clearly. But what we see is so grey that even to talk of socialism now seems utopian. Capitalist reality is closing in on us, rubbing out our hopes.

The very bleakness of the future that capitalism threatens us with makes it urgent that we ask again how we can make socialism. Without socialism we don't simply have a bad future ahead of us, we may have none at all.

Moving towards socialism

For as long as we can remember, the question of the transition to socialism has been polarised between two positions: on the one hand gradualism, on the other 'the seizure of state power'. But recently there seems to have been an increasing recognition that this debate is sterile. The obvious lack of possibilities for reform, coupled with our eye-opening experiences of 'participation', have disabused us of hopes in gradualism. There is no way that society can be transformed through institutions that have been developed precisely to take away our power.

On the other hand, a politics which pins everything on 'the seizure of state power' leaves many socialists feeling uncomfortable. They are sceptical about the possibility of overnight change, knowing it will be difficult to generate popular support for socialism when the question of just what it is we are fighting for is left so unreal. Neither capital nor the state can be seized, because they are not *things*. They are *relations* which cannot be grasped and held down, they have to be unmade. In a strange way our critique of the 'seizure of state power' line shares much with our doubts about gradualism: 'capturing power' by either means is not the same thing as taking control.

We need a socialist politics which both acknowledges that a

new society cannot be built through the old institutions *and* recognises that it cannot, either, be built in a single moment.

The gradualist way of thinking embraces ideas like 'progressive factory management' and 'good social work practice', while the smash-the-state way of thinking dismisses the idea that socialists should have anything to do (until after the revolution) with trying to change how factory work is organised or what happens in social work offices. We wrote *In and Against the State* because we felt that most socialists recognise that neither position is helpful to them in their everyday lives, as they try to contribute something themselves to the transition to socialism.

In the first edition we were trying to pose some alternative to these two unhelpful approaches. It hinges on the idea of *opposition*. The making of socialism is about taking every opportunity to counterpose our forms to theirs, in a way which undermines capital's social relations and at the same time prefigures what we would like to see.

Take health care, for instance. Socialist health care practice would include co-operative, non-hierarchical working relationships between health workers. It would mean sharing information and expertise between workers and with 'patients', creating opportunities for ill people to share their knowledge and experience. It would involve paying more attention to routine, everyday health care and finding ways of identifying and challenging the social causes of ill health. The struggle to establish these principles in however small a way, whether inside the NHS or outside it in mutual aid groups, has immediate benefits for both workers and 'patients'. But more important, it is also inevitably subversive. Capitalism's guilt for our ill health is obscured by the health service. To begin to take control of our own bodies and to ask what is making us ill is to undermine the institutional separation of what is making us ill from what purports to cure us.

In a similar way, socialist education practice, whether inside or outside the state, is about learning from experience and helping people to develop their capacity for asking questions and thinking critically. This is the kind of education we would like to see universally. But to the extent that we can also struggle for it now, it is threatening to the status quo.

Every time workers refuse to co-operate with the management's way of doing things, whether in the state or the private sector, the action is not just one of resistance; it must also involve working out what else to do instead. And the experience of working it out collectively can help develop our understanding of how decisions would be made in a socialist society. The principles and forms of organisation on which such oppositional practice is based and defended are precisely those which would form the basis for the new society.

To say all this is not to assert that the transition to socialism can be made without revolution. It is to recognise that there will be a continuity between the oppositional forms within the old society and the way the new society comes to be organised. It is much easier to conceive of creating a new society when we recognise that it can start with what we have built in opposing the old.

Embracing the revolutionary concept – that society cannot be transformed except as a whole and cannot be built through the old institutions – does *not* mean we have to engage in the kind of socialist politics which gives absolute priority to the pinnacles of class struggle – miners' strikes and the like. A socialist society cannot be created by 'bringing the government down' until such time as socialist practice is much more widespread and deep-rooted among us. The only realistic socialist practice is that of building a *culture of opposition*. By culture of opposition we do not mean culture in the narrow sense to do with people's forms of recreation, or indeed in the sense of 'alternative culture' of a few years ago. It is about infusing all aspects of everyday life, from work and health to child care and personal relationships, with oppositional practice.

But is there any hope for this kind of approach? Is there a way forward?

Fighting back

Although any account of capital's latest assault on us is inevitably depressing, there are dangers for capital too in the present situation. Intensified domination can give rise to fiercer resistance. New forms of ruling and oppressing us produce new ways of evading or fighting that rule and oppression. These are new risks for capital and new opportunities for socialists. The new mode of domination, which sometimes seems so confident, is really a desperate gamble on the part of capital. All of us are continually meeting with examples of resistance that show up in ways and places that never make the national headlines.

Joan, one of the Community Health Council workers, told us how the threatened closure of a clinic had produced resistance amongst the women using it. 'It was a beautiful place – friendly, non-authoritarian. The women using it really felt it to be their place. When the Area Health Authority said it was to be closed, the women in the Keep Fit class at the clinic started to organise. The AHA didn't know how to handle them – they were a real grass roots group, angry, unpredictable and uncontrollable. They had all sorts of imaginative ideas, like writing a collective poem and sending it to Jimmy Saville. And they won their fight. There was a confrontation over whether they might hang banners outside the clinic, in which the AHA had to back down. Eventually they said the clinic was to stay open.'

'I'll always remember what one of the women involved said to me: "I woke up in the middle of the night and suddenly everything became so clear to me that I wanted to write it down. I realised that life seems like a boxing match. It starts as soon as you have your kids. You take your kids to the clinic, but that's been closed. So you take them to another clinic and you have to wait so long that you never get to see the doctor. Then you take them to school and that has had cuts too. And finally when they're teenagers and start being troublesome they blame you for not looking after them properly!"'

As Joan said, 'the women felt they had to defend the clinic. They saw its closure as an assault on their whole lives.' Many, many other groups of people have been pushed into resistance by their anger in a similar way. But it is usually only when such struggles reach a national scale that we get to hear of them.

The insult of a two per cent pay offer turned steel workers, for instance, who for years had had to put up with one of the most moribund unions in Britain and with an industry bleeding to death, into a force that shook the Tories. The Tories had selected steel as their chosen nationalised industry battleground, where they could impose cuts in real pay, massive redundancies and intensified work. They didn't realise the force of the anger that would take the strike far beyond the leaders' moderating control.

The Corrie Bill made thousands of women forget the weariness of their years of marching against White and Benyon. London and other cities saw their largest demonstrations for years. They were determined demonstrations, knowing the seriousness of the threat, knowing that the anti-abortionists had a parliamentary majority, not daring to trust to blocking tactics in the House of Commons. Yet they had an oddly joyous feeling about them too. The joy arose from the realisation that the women's movement had built a force of opposition that could have gone on to contest Corrie in the clinics and in the surgeries if the right to abortion had been seriously curtailed in parliament.

The left provides no answers

So there is anger, and resistance, and even new opportunities for struggle. Yet these sparks of defiance have not rekindled the strength and confidence of the organised left. We might have expected the revolutionary groups to be flourishing. But many left organisations on the contrary seem to be having difficulty in keeping their membership from dwindling. Their slogans lack a direct appeal. There seems to be a gap between what they are saying and the reality of people's struggles, so that the two never quite make contact.

It is not surprising that there are not more adherents to a politics based on the concept of the 'once-upon-a-future' seizure of state power. This way of thinking doesn't seem to bear on the problems of everyday choice which we face as socialists within the state. It offers us no guidance as to how to handle these choices. It implies that the state is out there somewhere, external to us. We know that we are in it and entangled by relations in which we are personally implicated.

Feeling that the left groups are out of touch, many socialists – including lots who know all the arguments against 'reformism' and 'social democracy' – have joined the Labour Party. The left Labour councillors we talked to were feeling clear, in their own minds, that the reformist arguments and justifications that had brought them into the town hall were even less valid than they had been a year ago – resources were harder to come by, the scope of the management role had narrowed. Yet they reported an increase of membership in their local constituency parties of fifty per cent since the 1979 general election. These new members see the scale of the crisis and the attack on the working class, realise that they cannot fight it as individuals and want to join with others.

Mary and Patrick, two of the teachers we talked to, had recently joined the Labour Party with just this philosophy –

reluctantly, for lack of an alternative, feeling they must do *something*. And indeed this course does seem to offer the chance of impact. Particularly where local Labour Parties have been in decline. In such areas you do stand a chance of becoming a candidate in local elections within a year or two of joining.

Yet many like Mary and Patrick join the Labour Party with serious reservations. They reject what they feel to be the negativism of the left's analysis, but base their choice of engagement on the alternative theory of the state, with which they are equally ill at ease – the theory that tells us that the state is a ship we can sail to socialism, by infiltrating socialist members into the crew, trimming the rigging here and there, and using our own navigation charts.

In this way is created a to-and-fro effect in British politics, amply demonstrated since the second world war. A period of Tory government causes Labour to move left; Labour wins an election but moves right while in office; it is followed by yet another Tory government and so on. Somehow this alternating effect helps keep capitalism going by channelling our energy and anger into electioneering. The ship of state seems to sail the more calmly through capitalist waters just because it gets a periodic change of crew and tacks into each prevailing wind.

We have tried to demonstrate – through the interviews with people recounting their first hand experience of the state and in the analysis that followed – that the capitalist state is not a thing, nor even a set of things. This is why the metaphor of the ship – or even a fleet – will not do. The state is a complex set of relationships, relationships that individualise us, that deny the reality of class, that reinforce sexism and racism. As socialists we cannot be effective simply by seeking influence, trying to capture power, while offering no challenge to the form of class relations, just acting them out according to statute and precedent. We end up oppressing each other and confusing ourselves by doing so.

The fact that the Tories received the votes of many working-class people, especially in the South and Midlands of England, cannot be read as a manifestation of those people's 'false consciousness'. It is an accurate reflection of their real experience of social democracy and its promise of reform through the state. People do not any longer feel that the state is their friend – not even the welfare state. Not only has the state failed to deliver the goods (greater equality, full employment) but what goods it has delivered come to us in an oppressive, degrading, divisive form. So many working class people are prepared to go along – for their own reasons – with the ruling class rejection of an expanding state.

The Keynesian class strategy was most effective precisely in so far as it succeeded in imposing on many socialists a set of blinkers that denies this bad feeling people have about the state – 'statist' blinkers that led us into a 'statist' struggle, channelled exclusively through established institutional forms such as elections, parties, official trade union structures, formulations of social policy. The thrust of Keynesianism was to focus our attention on lobbying, council decisions, conference resolutions and so on – necessary as these are – to the neglect of the constant ferment of struggle that takes no institutional form and is often struggle *against* the state. The statist blinkers led us into 'participation' on every occasion that offered. Too often we used these openings, not for the oppositional possibilities they really did offer, which could have been exploited. Through them we were often lured into shouldering what were really *their* responsibilities in exchange for a phony share of power. Now monetarism has gained its freedom to operate, its political space, from the hidden weaknesses that the incorporation and institutionalisation of the Keynesian years have produced in those working class organisations that accepted it unquestioningly.

The hollowing out of our strength

We want to illustrate the kind of thing that has been happening to us by two cautionary tales. One is drawn from industry – British Leyland. The other example comes from the state – the demise of a law centre. This combination of 'private' and 'public' sectors is made purposefully, because it helps to emphasise that Keynesianism and monetarism are pervasive processes of class domination that influence our struggles everywhere. Taken together they demonstrate clearly that in fighting back against monetarism we must shed the 'statist' blinkers. It is no use stepping back and defending ourselves in the vocabulary Keynesianism taught us. We have to step forward and defend ourselves oppositionally.

During the post-war boom, the giant Longbridge plant of British Leyland developed one of the most powerful shop stewards organisations in Britain, jealous of its growing control over the organisation of work. In the sixties it was so strong that, in a situation of expanding markets, management had to adopt a conciliatory attitude to it, paying eight of the shop stewards to act effectively as full-time trade-union officials. Even after the firm first got into serious difficulties, this strategy of state-sponsored co-operation continued. The number of fulltime stewards was even increased from eight to fifty. Now they had their own management-provided offices and spent less and less time in contact with the shop floor. Increasingly, their job became one of mediating between management and the shop floor. Unwittingly they diffused resistance by channelling it through committee structures.

Management's strategy did not solve the company's financial problems: on the contrary they continued to grow. After Sir Michael Edwardes took over in 1977, a more vigorous assault began. This culminated in the submission to the company's workforce of a management plan for approval by secret ballot. Some union representatives published a pamphlet in opposition to the plan which, however, was overwhelmingly supported by the Leyland workforce. In November 1979 Derek Robinson, the convenor of the Longbridge stewards was sacked for having been one of the authors of the pamphlet. Attempts to organise industrial action in support of Robinson failed to achieve his reinstatement.

What had happened? A strong autonomous movement of workers was incorporated through its involvement in committees of management. This co-option helped make the counter-attack possible; 'participation' had offered the illusion of influence while actually undermining working class strength. In face of the monetarist assault this strength proved to have been hollowed out.

The British Leyland story is a microcosm of the seventies: a period of working class strength and militancy is followed by a period of concession and incorporation. It was a risky and a costly strategy for capital and it made a new assault necessary. But it also laid the ground for that assault – because when it came, working class organisations were no longer rooted in real strength.

The second example of this same process is one of many that could be cited from our dealings with the local state. In chapter 1 we talked to some workers in a local authority-funded law centre. We talked to them again recently – a year later. All three law centres in their borough had been closed down. What was interesting was the way their very institutional nature and relationship with the state had impeded them when it came to putting up a fight. The local authority increasingly criticised them for acting 'politically', for working with groups, for failing to 'sit in the office and run a cost-effective walk-in service for individuals'.

When the threat of closure came, the law centre workers found themselves defending their centres within the council's own terms of reference, trying to prove their usefulness and efficiency. 'Looking back, we can see we were led along the garden path by the council. We made one compromise after another in the hope of staying alive. We kept justifying ourselves to them, trying to prove that we were really doing what they wanted. But we were closed down in the end. We should have realised what was happening sooner and made a more constructive struggle, doing what *we* wanted to do with the money we had left, doing what best reflected working class people's need in our area.'

There are countless other examples of struggle gone wrong, littered along the road from rising working class strength of the early seventies to the defeat and demoralisation of 1979 and 1980. The lesson of all the stories is the same: to pursue power by winning positions of influence for the working class *within the terms of the state form of social relations* is mistaken.

The working class is present in the state in numberless positions and numberless ways. But to be present in formal positions of responsibility or power is different from being present in struggle. Working class presence within the state's own form of relations is a hollow strength. It is this hollowness which has allowed the 'new right' to come in, not with any massive social support (in this it differs from fascism), but with a negative social base of mistrust and distaste for the state.

We can cite three examples of the ways in which our experience of the monetarist mode of domination is pushing us to change the way we see our relationship, as socialists, with the state.

Take, first, the present threat to many clerical and administrative jobs in the civil service and local government. In these jobs we have a choice about the kind of campaign we wage in our own defence, similar in many ways to the choice we have in our 'welfare' jobs. We can adopt oppositional strategies that challenge the official purpose of our work, the relations of control within it and its effect on the working class outside it, countering those things with our own socialist conception of what this work could and should be. Or we can wage a defensive, sectional struggle to secure our jobs and improve our pay and status within the terms of the state's own form of relations. If we do this, we will elicit little support from a working class that shares the Tory distaste for 'too many officials' and 'too much red tape'.

Secondly, we have seen that one aspect of the new mode of domination is to reduce the number of paid workers in the 'caring' jobs of the state and to appeal instead for volunteers. As socialists we often react to this by rejecting the idea of volunteer work out of hand, both in order to defend state jobs and to pin on the state what we have come to feel are its proper responsibilities. In many circumstances this is right. But perhaps we also ought to step outside the official uses of 'public' and 'private'. Many people, from hard experience, have come to identify official services with being put down, with lack of care, and on the contrary to value help voluntarily given as being somehow more humane. Our future struggle, as socialists and feminists, has to move on from the narrow concept that 'if it is socialist it must always be state'. We have to fight for what we need of the state. But at the same time we can develop strategies whereby unpaid action becomes, and can be seen to be, struggle not charity. For instance, when women share their skills and experience in self-help health groups this can become the basis for a fight for better state health care.

Thirdly, looking ahead, it is possible to see that similar dangers in dependence on state and state forms of action arise in relation to the campaigns against the cuts. Several left-wing Labour councils are refusing to implement the cuts. This is to be welcomed. But all such councils to date have continued to take responsibility for managing the crisis – by increasing rates by as much as forty per cent. In this way the working class pays for the crisis in an alternative way.

Too often even the most left-wing Labour councillors see the battle as taking place within the council chamber rather than in the schools and the housing estates. 'Power' of this kind – the 'influence' the working class gained through parliamentarism and managerialism – can sometimes be a trap. For Labour councils, just as much as Tory councils, are experienced by most people as the enemy, as the oppressor, as the body that won't provide decent housing or repair what exists, that keeps children out of nurseries and refuses to pay decent wages to its workers.

When the crunch comes, when Whitehall's commissioners

move in to deal with the over-spending, will people in these areas unite to protect the councils that defended 'their' services? We hope so, but we fear not. For the very way in which services are provided, to individual patients, parents, clients – militates against collective organisation to defend them. And, as we have said many times, they are not in any case seen as *our* services, while the money we have to pay out in increased rates is very clearly *our* money.

Search for new forms

The failure in socialist organisations and strategic thinking, however, has its good side as well as its bad. There is a new openness around. Nowadays you have to delude yourself very badly if you want to think you have all the answers. For example, a book written by three socialist feminists, *Beyond the Fragments*, has, by its questioning of standard left assumptions, created more of a stir than any similar work for many years. It has had its impact, not because it provides answers that will solve all our problems, but because it raises questions that many people were asking silently. How can we act on what we learned from the sixties and seventies, from new movements, particularly from the women's movement? What can we do about the fact that many of us, as committed socialists, find exisiting socialist organisations inadequate?

Anger, energy, opposition on the one hand – absence of a strong, organised movement on the other. Why is there this gap? Our central point is that we cannot seek the answer in the 'apathy' of those who do not join the organised left. We must look rather to our own practices as socialists for an answer. We have to ask not 'what is wrong with all these people that they aren't joining in our struggle?', but 'what is it about the way we are organising, the way the issues are raised, the vision offered, that makes it inadequate as a basis for mass action?'. For it is not that people are unwilling to resist. Resistance is all around. It does not always take recognised traditional forms like strikes. Sabotage on the assembly line, truancy from school, women walking out of oppressive marriages – all these are resistance.

What is wrong is surely that our existing trade unions and socialist institutions fail even to perceive, much less to help collectivise, all the thousand acts of everyday resistance. Our organisations too often do not speak to people's predicament, listen to what they want, reflect their pent-up anger.

Our problem then is to find effective forms of struggle with which to respond to capital's offensive. We have to understand what precisely it is that we are up against, to think of ways in which forms of resistance can be collectivised and assisted, and to think how we can transform this resistance to capitalism into the achievement of socialism.

The call for a renewed reliance on traditional trade union and labour party politics is partly based on the misconception that what we are experiencing now is a return to the thirties. We have already pointed out some of the ways the emerging situation differs from the pre-war decades. Now there is an entirely new technology of control, from nuclear power to psychotropic drugs, a new mode of domination, different groups of people bearing the brunt of capital's offensive – in particular black people (scarcely present in the UK before the war), women, school leavers, pensioners. There are new issues and new groups at the focal points of class struggle.

The old forms of organisation simply have not adapted to the new circumstances – not that they ever did give adequate expression to the anger of many groups. New forms of struggle are needed which answer to the needs of *everyone* involved, both in terms of appropriate forms of organisation and of defining what it is we are fighting for.

Take women as an instance – since half of us writing this are women. We are the ones who will be expected to cope as living standards fall and nurseries, hospitals and old people's homes close down. It is also women who are losing their jobs fastest and who may well turn out to be at the core of the struggle over the new technology. What autonomy and control over their own fertility women have succeeded in establishing over the last few years is also being undermined. For these reasons it is now quite impossible to conceive of a movement of mass resistance to capital's offensive which does not have women at the centre, especially when it comes to struggles in and against the state.

All of this is nominally recognised by socialists. Yet too often men, and sometimes women too, see the problem as one of 'how to draw women in'. We think this is to pose the question the wrong way round. What we need to ask is how can we rethink and change both what it is we are fighting for as socialists, and our way of fighting for it, so that both match the needs of those of us who are women.

Those whose history has been in the labour movement are steeped in a form of organising that has been developed primarily by men, with committees, delegate structures, representatives, negotiators and so on, procedures and roles in which women often feel at a loss. Women however are not without characteristic ways of organising – many have brought much courage and inventiveness to direct action, in Ireland, in urban communities. Women also have more experience than men of working co-operatively, especially in small, mutually supportive groups.

Nor are women as passive as is often assumed. Women are struggling all the time. Making ends meet, pressing for a nursery place, securing an exceptional needs payment, getting the electricity reconnected, trying to stop the children being taken away, securing an adequate share of the wage for housekeeping. The problem is that women's many bitter struggles are often very isolated and individual ones. They are often in the family, often take the form of a struggle against a man, or men, in the home. The problem is to find ways of de-individualising these struggles and strengthening collective organisation where it does exist.

Beyond questions of organisation, however, we should recognise that almost all these issues that concern women involve deep rooted and complicated feelings. The cuts, for instance, often affect nurseries, homes and hospitals which look after people who would otherwise be looked after by their families. Socialists oppose the closure of these institutions: caring for dependent relatives at home can impose intolerable burdens and there is no reason why this should be women's unpaid work. At the same time we must recognise that having our relatives cared for by the state often involves deeply ambiguous feelings, including guilt about admitting there are limits to our loving and caring and anxiety about poor standards of care. For these reasons slogans like 'We refuse to cope' are unlikely to mobilise many women. In this kind of situation we need to find ways of organising that don't trample on our feelings, which face up to and work through the contradictions.

These are just some examples of the problems and possibilities inherent in the struggle of women. We have not written about other kinds of situation– because as it happens none of us is a teenager, none of us is a pensioner, none of us is unemployed at the time of writing, none of us is black. We sense that similar questions are being asked by all these and other groups of people – questions about how to develop appropriate forms of struggle which build on the strengths of their own traditions of organising, whether formal or informal, and accurately reflect their predicament.

In discussions of the first edition of *In and Against the State*, people have sometimes said 'You've put forward a collection of tactics for everyday struggle, but where is your strategy for the transition to socialism?'

We do not have a strategy to offer, nor is it appropriate that we should. Small groups of socialists spend too much time trying to think up strategies in isolation. We do not need a 'line'. More important is to develop a tentative feeling for principles – sensitive to differing, varied experiences of capital and the state – that can help those of us who feel tied up in the oppressive relations of capitalism, collectively to choose forms of everyday opposition to it. The guidelines already exist, we have brought them out of our recent history.

Holding to what we have learned

We must not let go of the understanding of capitalism and the state that we acquired so painfully during the Keynesian decades. As the crisis deepens and many socialists call for a return to the traditional politics of the labour movement, a rallying to the Labour Party, a return to industry, we must hold on to what we have learned – in the squatting movement, the women's movement, in actions as diverse as Rock Against Racism and community publishing. In particular there are four crucial points.

1. Socialist practice must be rooted in people's own experience.

What we have learned, particularly from the women's movement, is that our struggle is strongest when it is based on a shared understanding of what brings people to the struggle in the first place, when our forms of action correspond to the personal needs of those involved. We have learned, too, that paying attention to the complexities and contradictions in people's lives will in the long run be a source of strength. People's views and feelings cannot simply be dismissed as 'false consciousness'. There are often coherent and plausible reasons why people turn to private medicine or want to

buy their council house. Unless we listen to these and take account
of them in formulating a socialist approach to health care, or
housing, as the case may be, it is quite unlikely that we will ever be
able to build a mass movement.

We have been saying that the capitalist state individualises
people, that it denies the fact that we have a common problem and
in doing so undermines our potential collective strength. We have
to accept, then, that people *are* divided. People are racist and sexist,
we often blame and fight each other rather than capitalism and
those who control it. We cannot write people off for turning against
each other, pensioners for hating punks, or punks for hating
pensioners. We have to find ways of bringing them into a shared
struggle.

2. Socialism cannot be built without a vision of what is possible.

In the past we have sometimes thought that if only we explain to
people that their problems arise from living in a capitalist society,
this alone will be enough to bring them to a commitment to
socialism. It is increasingly clear, however, that people's commitment to fight back is in part related to the extent to which they
can see a way out. We know this from our own experience: it is the
glimpses of how it *could* be - gained in many of the 'alternatives' of
the late sixties and early seventies - that keep us going. The
unpalatable fact is that for most people socialism means nothing
better than the monolith of Soviet Russia, or the drabness of the
welfare state writ large. It is hardly surprising that it does not have a
lot of popular appeal.

At the moment it is the radical right who are making all the
running when it comes to 'new values'. Meanwhile, for most people,
socialism is associated with a defence of the post war status quo. It
doesn't have to be like this. Socialists could stop being afraid to
paint a picture of what they want to see, afraid of being accused of
being utopian or unrealistic. We need to talk about what we are
working for - about a life where we can be free of the fear of war,
where we have time for ourselves and the people we care for, where
we can live in unpolluted places and uncrowded houses, eat good
food and enjoy good health. We know what we want to have - a
society where each person can be equally valued, equally in control
- and it is necessary to spell it out, to imagine it, to make it real. The
most tangible way to do it is through the relations we choose to build

in our struggles now. We can value and emphasise those aspects of our struggles that prefigure and begin to build the kind of world we want.

A hospital campaign, say, need not be a merely rhetorical defence of an institution which people never really felt was theirs anyway. Hospital occupations have been made into opportunities to try out new ways in which hospital workers of different kinds, workers and patients, workers and community, can relate to each other, giving a glimpse of how it could be. Besides, many more people will be willing to throw their strength behind a struggle of this kind.

It seems clear to us that socialism is only made in the course of resistance. Our own ways of doing things can only be developed as we unmake the relations of capital. But resistance is more than the refusal to be dominated. It is also about positively asserting how things could be. For too long socialists have been silent about what it is all our struggles are *for*. We should break the silence.

3. Our whole lives are subject to capitalism.

In the last decade we have learned that the personal is political. We have found that capitalist domination penetrates every aspect of our lives: schools, hospitals, the law, technology, what we eat, even the air we breathe. Through the interlocking systems of male supremacy, of racial domination and religious authority with the oppressive structures of capitalism, our most personal domestic relationships are deformed. There is no politics-free zone.

This insight is fundamental for our politics. Our concern is no longer simply to eliminate injustices and anomalies. It is not even about scandals and horror stories. We do not need to seek out extreme cases of police brutality or starving children to demonstrate the evils of capitalism. We can simply recount to ourselves our everyday experience of oppression. Our struggle is about everyday opposition to the *normal condition of things*.

*4. Socialism is about transforming power relations,
not about capturing power.*

One sure thing we have found out from all the 'participation' exercises of the Keynesian years, whether it was a matter of tenants co-opted to the housing committee, the TUC sitting at the table with the government, or left Labour MPs voted into parliament;

getting 'our' people into 'their' structures rarely brings the gains we hoped for. Worse, in complicated and subtle ways, it somehow actually reinforces our powerlessness and confuses our struggle. However excellent the socialist credentials of the people who have taken their place in these structures they have only been able to make an impact when they have challenged their terms of reference or forms of organisation.

Lenin said that power was a question of 'who/whom'. We have learned that this is not quite right. It is not just a question of *who* dominates *whom*: it is more a question of *how*. Or rather, it is that the question of who dominates cannot be separated from the form of domination.

Power is maintained in our society not because there are unpleasant individuals in control whose interests are not our interests, but because the *relations of control* have been shaped by capital in its own image. Our struggle is therefore in part the assertion of our own ways of doing things, ways which are rooted in people's lived experience rather than betraying it, ways that strengthen rather than whittle away people's confidence, and foster collectivity rather than individualism.

The hopeful thing about the passage of the last ten or fifteen years is that we have had some very positive as well as negative experiences on this question of power. For instance, squatters dramatised homelessness not by getting their elected representative onto the council's housing committee, but by practical action which challenged the relations of property itself, contested the fact that the value of houses arises from their standing empty, claimed instead that it rests in their potential for use.

People sometimes say that women have no power because they are not well represented in the trade unions, in the parties or in parliament. And of course this is partly true. But the women's movement did not seek seats in the House of Commons because women were finding a different sense of power, their own power. We were coming to realise that our oppression partly arises from the way we have been divided from each other and that the first blow in fighting back is to reassert our own collectivity.

The process in the health movement has been similar: we have gained strength to confront the experts by sharing our personal experience, learning about our own bodies and discovering common patterns in our illness and our interactions with the health service.

In each of these situations we have made positive gains not by 'winning power' in any formal sense but by taking a degree of control, counter-posing our forms of organisation to theirs. From practical experiences in struggle, not just from utopian dreaming, we have concluded that we must forge our own forms of organisation. Not just because it is more congenial but in order to win – by challenging and eroding the power of capital over our lives. And not just to defeat capital but to build socialism – because a struggle waged in our own way is the only possible point of departure for a world we can live in on our own terms. The future must be ours not theirs and we must be making it now.

Lesley Doyal with Imogen Pennell

The Political Economy of Health

Ill-health and disease are generally seen as misfortunes which just happen to people and which scientific medicine is on the point of eliminating – or at least dedicated to combatting. In *The Political Economy of Health* the authors question these views in fundamental ways. They show that ill-health, in both developed and underdeveloped countries, is largely a product of the social and economic organisation of society. They show that medical practice and research are strongly influenced by their role in maintaining a healthy labour force and in socialising and controlling people, and that the medical field provides a large and growing arena for the accumulation of capital.

A critique of sociological approaches sets the framework for exploring these ideas in detail. Among other things the authors look at:

Changing patterns of health and illness and the development of medical practice in Britain and the Third World, highlighting the relationship between imperialism, medicine and underdevelopment.

The relationship between medicine and medical ideology and the oppression of women

The problems of socialised medicine under capitalism and the present crisis in the NHS in Britain.

The book concludes with a discussion of the significance of political struggles relating to medicine and health.

Lesley Doyal is a Senior Lecturer and Imogen Pennell is a research worker at the Polytechnic of North London. They are both involved in the women's health movement and in the Politics of Health Group.

0 86104 074 0 paperback   0 86104 075 9 hardback

Andrew Glyn and John Harrison

The British Economic Disaster

Andrew Glyn and John Harrison focus on two points where left
and right in British politics agree: that the country's long
economic decline has become a disaster and that our central
political problem is how to avoid its consequences.

The authors trace the development of the current crisis since
the war. They show how both Labour and Tory governments
compounded the effect of a declining world boom. They review
the 'extreme' solutions now on offer to the public: Thatcherite
monetarism and the Bennite 'alternative economic strategy'.
And they find both woefully inadequate to the task their
proponents set themselves: how to save the British economy
from ruin when the oil runs out. In conclusion the authors
propose a far-reaching programme for social and economic
change in Britain.

Andrew Glyn is co-author, with Bob Sutcliffe, of *British
Capitalism, Workers and the Profits Squeeze.* John Harrison is the
author of *Marxist Economics for Socialists.*

ISBN 0 86104 317 0 paperback only